CU00825955

"Precious few books combine practical ;
sights into academic finance theory and
Dividend is one of them. Daniel Peris of
history of dividend investing, puncturin
along the way—an important contributic

"Daniel Peris powerfully combines a practitioner's experience with extraor-
dinary analytical perspective on the evolution and likely future course of
dividends as a determinant of investment returns. Investors and money
managers owe it to themselves to challenge their assumptions by very care-
fully studying every page of this book."

"Peris presents not only a comprehensive theory for understanding the art
of investing under conditions of uncertainty, but he also makes the case for
cashflow-based investing, which he argues compellingly will come increasingly back into favor in the years to come. His contributions to the field
of dividend-based investing should be made mandatory study for financial
professionals and novices alike."

"The media and Wall Street are obsessed with market values, and that obsession has led the investing public to downgrade the importance of dividends. This is a mistake! Dividends are the more stable and more secure
source of investment returns. Furthermore, paying dividends forces corporations to be more thoughtful about their capital allocation decisions.
Daniel Peris has written an interesting and important book. Wall Street,
corporate executives, and the investing public should pay attention."

"Daniel Peris takes you deep into the history of dividend investing. Dividends were once the largest component of investment returns; after 1980
that slowly ceased to be true. Now the market appears to be on the verge
of another major transition. This book explains the factors driving that
change."

THE OWNERSHIP DIVIDEND

We are on the verge of a major paradigm shift for investors in the U.S. stock market. Dividend-focused stock investing has been receding in popularity for more than three decades in the United States; once the dominant investment style, it is now a boutique approach. That is about to change.

The Ownership Dividend explains how and why the stock market drifted away from a mostly cash-based returns system to one almost completely driven by near-term share price movements. It details why the exceptional forces behind that shift—notably the 40-year drop in interest rates and the rise of buybacks—are now substantially exhausted. As a result, the U.S. market is poised for a return to the more typical business-like relationships observed in the private sector and in other mature markets around the world. While many market participants have profited from and become used to the way things have been in recent decades, savvy individual investors, financial advisors, and even institutional portfolio managers will want to position themselves to benefit from the reversion to cash-based investment relationships in the years ahead.

This is a must-read book for financial advisors and institutional consultants, as well as engaged individual investors.

Daniel Peris oversees dividend-focused portfolios for Federated Hermes in Pittsburgh. Initially trained as a historian, he is the author of three books on investing as well as a study of the former Soviet Union.

THE OWNERSHIP DIVIDEND

The Coming Paradigm Shift in the U.S. Stock Market

Daniel Peris

LONDON AND NEW YORK

Designed cover image: Getty Images/champc

First published 2024
by Routledge
4 Park Square, Milton Park, Abingdon, Oxon OX14 4RN

and by Routledge
605 Third Avenue, New York, NY 10158

Routledge is an imprint of the Taylor & Francis Group, an informa business

British Library Cataloguing-in-Publication Data
A catalogue record for this book is available from the British Library

ISBN: 978-1-032-27052-4 (hbk)
ISBN: 978-1-032-27319-8 (pbk)
ISBN: 978-1-003-29227-2 (ebk)

DOI: 10.4324/9781003292272

Typeset in Garamond
by Apex CoVantage, LLC

CONTENTS

PREFACE

In the past dozen years, I've written three books on investing. Two were focused on dividends; one was a historical critique of Modern Portfolio Theory. It's a fair question as to why I do this. It's certainly not for the money. Few books make their authors wealthy. They may help as tools to market the financial products I manage, but the time involved in writing them is vast, and there is no guarantee that any incremental business would ever cover that cost. If not for royalties or new business, readers might assume that I write books to show off what I know. That may be the motivation of other practitioner authors, but in my case, the opposite is true: I write not to demonstrate expertise to the reader, but to force me, as a practitioner, to master the material of my trade.

When I entered the asset management industry 25 years ago from an entirely different career, I quickly memorized the formulas, picked up a certification to show basic competence, and went on my way. But it soon dawned on me that such preparation—and the on-the-job training I received the first few years—was woefully insufficient. First, the style in which I invested was so out-of-fashion that it was barely included in the canon. Either the industry instruction was wrong or I was misguided. It needed to be investigated. Second, having been trained as an academic historian, I was struck by how ahistorical the investment profession is. With a few exceptions—the occasional wizened old soul—most investors have limited time horizons, both forward and backward. That was not for me. So I set about actually learning about dividend investing. And for me, there is no better way to master a topic than to write about it. Putting an extended, complex argument on paper forces you to think through all the angles, address the weaknesses, get the sequence right, confront logical flaws in your thinking, wrestle with data that might not agree with your hypothesis, and otherwise generally challenge your work. What the writing exercise does not uncover—in terms of weaknesses—the editing process does.

A critic could point out that book publishing is hard and time-consuming. Why not just do the research and writing but leave the publishing to the "Get Rich Quick!" schemers? It's a fair point, but putting the material in the public space—whether as a traditionally published book or as new media—raises the stakes quite a bit. It forces even greater analysis and review. Decision-making under conditions of uncertainty can never be exact, despite the academics dressing it up as a science. There is always some risk of being "wrong" in some matter of analysis or interpretation, but that is a risk I am willing to take. Complete empirical accuracy is not as important as the broader logic attending it. Consider this then a disclaimer: "This is not investment advice. It may or may not be correct. Consult your financial advisor before making any investment decisions, etc."

INTRODUCTION

Books on investing are usually about the next big thing, often an emerging technology, perhaps a trading strategy, or a prediction of a market boom or bust. Publishers prefer these works to be "actionable," with specific investing recommendations. But the next big thing can easily be structural. The emergence of Modern Portfolio Theory in the 1950s and 1960s was one example. The creation of a practical index fund in 1975 was another. The same is true with the 1982 change in SEC rules that permitted the now ubiquitous share buyback programs. These shifts may not have fit the model of "how to make a million in the next twelve months," but they ended up involving trillions, not millions, of dollars over subsequent decades. That's another definition of actionable: how to think about the stock market and position your portfolio for changes likely to occur in the years ahead.

One such moment is upon us. For most of its history, the stock market was based on a presumed and usually an actual cash relationship between companies and their owners, particularly for larger, more successful businesses. That is, those enterprises paid dividends to their shareholders. In that regard, the relationship was consistent with what someone with a stake in any successful

DOI: 10.4324/9781003292272-1

ongoing business might expect from their holding. They would receive their share of the profits after all the operating expenses and future investment needs of the venture had been met. Consider that a maxim of business ownership. Despite that foundational understanding of investment, dividend-focused stock investing has been receding in popularity for more than three decades in the United States. Once the necessarily dominant investment style, it is now a boutique approach. This book explains how and why the stock market drifted away from a mostly cash-based returns system to one almost completely driven by near-term share price movements. It details why I believe the forces behind that shift are now substantially exhausted. As a result, the U.S. market is poised to return to the more typical businesslike relationships observed in the private sector and in other mature markets around the world. While many market participants have gotten used to (and profited from) the way things have been in recent decades, savvy individual investors, financial advisors, and even institutional portfolio managers will want to benefit from the reversion to cash-based investment relationships in the years ahead.

Claiming that a paradigm shift in a major facet of modern American society is about to occur is necessarily a polemical endeavor. It involves making essentially unprovable assertions about the future based on a selected reading from the past. It will be years, if not decades, before we know for certain whether the claim was correct. Moreover, shifts in major paradigms are hard to identify from within. The natural tendency is to assume the continuation of current beliefs and practices. That is the very nature of a paradigm. The changes argued for here may be controversial for the additional reason that the empirical evidence has been going almost entirely in the opposite direction for several decades. The current cashless approach to the U.S. stock market holds all the high ground.

The rise and crash of the dot-com stocks at the turn of the millennium is not the issue. In the two decades since, a crop of very successful, highly profitable, abundantly cash-generating, and even mature companies have come to dominate the investment landscape. (Today, there are neo-dot-coms, in the form of SPACs, but they are a sideshow.) That these companies still do not have a cash relationship with their owners is the matter. It is a clear, if not the clearest, manifestation of the current paradigm. And yet, no one raises an eyebrow that these companies that we all use every day do not pay dividends to their owners. In part that is because the currently dominant investment narrative celebrates large successful enterprises not sharing their good fortune with company owners. It is the almost complete acceptance of this approach that I wish to call out and challenge.

The lack of concern by most investors is understandable if you consider that essentially everyone under the age of 67 reading this book (in 2024) has known just the single investing environment of declining interest rates and diminishing and then very low cash returns from stocks. For those individuals working in finance today—the CFA charterholders and MBA graduates, almost all CFOs and corporate treasurers, and the vast majority of investment bankers, strategy consultants, risk managers, pundits, and active investors—the sharp rise in rates in 2022 is nearly foreign territory.[1] Their singular experience is complemented by the complete stranglehold of the current approach to investing in the academy and professional training, as well as the interests of brokers and the media. Two full generations into this paradigm, it will be an uphill struggle to convince investors, practitioners, and corporate executives that a change is about to occur.

Is there an effort to nudge history along, in the spirit of Robert Shiller's narrative economics, by talking enough about a paradigm shift, that, were the story to go "viral," it would actually take place?[2] Perhaps, but I do not flatter myself as to having such an impact on the capital markets. And I grant that critics will likely agree that a paradigm shift occurred, but that it was in the 1990s when U.S. stocks began moving in the direction of becoming nearly cashless investments. By that line of thinking, a return to what I call normal business relations is not in the cards. They will say that I am fighting the last war, which was soundly won by their side. Other, younger critics will acknowledge that a paradigm shift is underway but that it is one that involves moving in an entirely different direction, toward an investment climate based on alternative digital currencies, specifically those relying on decentralized ledger technologies rather than government-based fiat money. Well, we shall see.

In contrast to those views, the premise here is that the underlying cash basis of commerce and investment is fundamental. Whether that occurs with strings of beads, blocks of salt, gold coins, dollars, or some other widely accepted means of exchange, this book lays out why sooner or later—and probably sooner—those more normal business relations will reassert themselves in the U.S. stock market. I acknowledge the burden of an out-of-consensus view. Though I have hundreds of years of modern economic activity and literally millions of real-world businesses on my side of the equation, the current paradigm has the last 30 years of the U.S. stock market ecosystem on its side. For current market participants, their "recency bias" will be hard to overcome. Be that as it may, the lines have been drawn. In that regard, my proposed "mean reversion" in capital markets relationships is, in effect, the second exercise in narrative finance on this topic. The first tale that was told and went viral is the one that we have observed for the past 30 years—that large, successful businesses would not necessarily make profit distributions to their company owners. This work argues for a new narrative, one that both hearkens back to prior business fundamentals, but positions the investor for a market framework based on what will be a renewed cash nexus between investor and investment.

The upcoming shift will benefit two audiences. The first is the formerly endangered species to which I belong: those who want a cash-based (as opposed to just price-based) relationship with their assets, whether those assets are real estate, private businesses, or even publicly traded stocks. One goal is to help those individuals sleep better at night, safe in the knowledge that they are of "sound mind" when they consider their approach to investing, and to argue, more practically, that they are likely to see some relief in the years to come. That is to say, more companies will pay larger dividends, and dividend investors will have a much larger opportunity set, than they do currently. While acknowledging that a realignment in the structure of the stock market creates profitable opportunities for those who are prepared, I also view this effort as a public service announcement for the long-suffering widows-and-orphans traditional investor. I had the pleasure of watching Louis

Rukeyser's *Wall Street Week* on PBS when I was much younger. I would like to consider this a small payback for his contributions to the art of clarity and common sense. They are what make for genuine sleep-at-night investing.

For the other, much larger group of investors not in the self-selecting cash group, the goal is perhaps even more important—to point out that the current investment framework is a choice, not an inevitability. They have an opportunity to prepare for the move away from what I called in an earlier work "the casino" to a more businesslike approach to publicly traded enterprises. Moreover, most investors are aware that the best time to embrace a particular investment style is not when it is in favor, but when it is out of favor. And an even better time to do it is when the style is really out of favor, three decades out of favor. And that's where we are presently.

Given that I've written several books on investing over the past dozen years, why this new effort?[3] First and most importantly, after a multi-decade decline in perceived investment risk, the likelihood of a further sustained move lower is minimal. The rise in interest rates that occurred in 2022 may or may not be maintained, but it is clear that the long downtrend in risk rates—the real-world sense of genuine business and investment risk—has been broken. Now is the time to point out the implications of that major development. The second reason I'm writing this book is that post-COVID-19, many commentators have suggested that the "old" has been irreversibly shuffled out in favor of work-from-home, super supply chain wizards, and anything using Artificial Intelligence (AI). Perhaps, but I will argue that for all the hoopla and excitement that we are experiencing, the clear-headed business investor needs to stick to the basics. COVID-19 and the resulting shocks to the global economy present an opportunity to review and refresh the basics of investing, not fundamentally change them. The virtues of clarity do not change as a result of a crisis; indeed, they are strengthened.

The first part of *The Ownership Dividend* sets the stage for how the current, anomalous situation in regard to stocks came about. Chapter 1 outlines the stock market environment from its earliest beginnings to the 1950s or so. Chapter 2 traces the intellectual and academic lineage of the move to dividend-free and dividend-light stocks. Chapter 3 tracks the three main forces that drove the market's transition: declining interest rates, the rise of the share buyback, and the emergence of Nasdaq and Silicon Valley. Chapter 4 summarizes investing for dividends in the constrained environment of the past several decades.

The second part of *The Ownership Dividend* is forward-looking. Chapter 5 presents what I regard as the key philosophical underpinnings of investing in the stock market. Notably, they have little to do with valuation, security selection, portfolio management, etc. Instead, it is about knowing what you want. I frame it as a battle between two forces. The first is the industry's official, one-size-fits-all canonical "Truth" as to what you should want from the market. The second is your personal and unique version of sleep-at-night Clarity when it comes to investing. They are far from being the same. Chapter 6 revisits cashflow-based investing from that minority of the academy that did not dismiss dividends as irrelevant and outdated. Chapter 7 highlights what is and will be different in stock investing when the cash nexus has returned. Chapter 8 suggests some adjustments to how we measure and track investments given the changes in the investing climate. Chapter 9 takes up the thorny and controversial issues of sustainable investing within the broader context of our abruptly shifting political economy. I do not go deep into this rabbit hole because it is so intriguing and involved that I would probably never make it out. Chapter 10 takes the first steps toward portfolio positioning in the coming environment. As each investor is different, it is meant to be suggestive, not exhaustive.

When I started this project in 2020, interest rates were still continuing their long march down. Benefitting from a near-zero cost of cash money and genuine risk rates at or below zero, "fancy" stocks, SPACs, unicorns, and all sorts of exotic financial animals on boats were all the rage. The first half of the book was written in that environment. The second half was written after rates had risen sharply in 2022. My original intent was to forecast a capital market environment that would come into being sometime in the future. I was late and missed the turning point. One year does not a paradigm make, and while I wish this work had come out prior to the move-up in rates, it is clearly not too late to make my points. This paradigm shift will play out over years and decades, not months.

At around 60,000 words, this work is meant for practitioners, not academics. Topics not covered in sufficient depth for any given reader can be pursued "offline" by reaching me via my website (www.strategicdividendinvestor.com) or via social media. By definition, a traditional printed book is a static source of information and data. Fortunately, the digital age permits easy updating. In that spirit, much of the data referenced in the text will be presented, maintained, and updated on my website for as long as is practical.[4] And I will continue to address many of the issues raised here on my various social media platforms. I look forward to exchanges with engaged readers.

NOTES

[1] Those born before 1957—and were therefore at least 25 at the highpoint of rates in 1982—might have some memory and professional experience of rising rates and high inflation.

[2] Robert J. Shiller, *Narrative Economics: How Stories Go Viral and Drive Major Economic Events* (Princeton: Princeton University Press, 2019).

[3] Daniel Peris, *The Strategic Dividend Investor* (New York: McGraw-Hill, 2011); *The Dividend Imperative* (New York: McGraw-Hill, 2013); *Getting Back to Business* (New York: McGraw-Hill, 2018).

[4] https://strategicdividendinvestor.com/the-ownership-dividend-charts-and-tables/.

1

RAISING CAPITAL, EARNING PROFITS, PAYING DIVIDENDS

From the inception of modern stock markets until the most recent period, dividends played a foundational role in the investing experience of most investors. While the dividends themselves took many shapes and forms, the popular narratives around investing usually concerned the timely payment of dividends. The academic study of the capital markets for prior periods depends substantially on the history of company dividend payments. Many elements of stock investing—taxation of dividends, breadth of ownership, the buyback phenomenon, etc.—have changed over the years, but the foundational nature of dividends for investors in the U.S. stock market until around 30 years ago is undeniable.

IN THE BEGINNING ...

In the beginning ... there was the *Vereenigde Oost Indische Compagnie* or VOC.[1] That's not actually true. There were prior joint-stock companies, but as a practical matter, the Dutch East India Company was the first recognizable stock traded on the

DOI: 10.4324/9781003292272-2

purpose-designed Amsterdam exchange. *From that exchange's launch in 1602 until the mid-20th century, investment in a stock like VOC was—in most instances for most people—all about the dividend that investors could expect to receive.*[2] That is not to suggest that money was not made and lost on pure price speculations, frauds, bubbles, struggling enterprises, and all sorts of other investment decisions and holding experiences. Those non-dividend moments are unavoidable when stocks trade daily and dividend payments or changes are made quarterly or annually. But weigh those headline-dominating moments, and they pale in comparison to the much quieter but vastly greater experience of regular coupon clipping. From that perspective, it is clear that the dividend was the ultimate measure of a stock's long-term success. If the dividend was paid, that was good. If it was increased, that was better. Over the long term, share prices reflected the trajectory of the dividend, plus or minus sentiment factors that influenced the cash yield that was acceptable to investors. Real returns—those adjusted for inflation – suggest that the cash dividend received in any given period was much if not all of the real return for that period, given that inflation and dividend growth would largely offset one another. In addition, for almost all of this period until well into the 20th century, the dividend was often the only public information (beyond the share price) one might be able to get about a traded company. Regular, audited, and standardized financial statements came much, much later.

THE NARRATIVE OF STOCKS AND DIVIDENDS

The self-proclaimed "science" of investment emerged only in the early to mid-20th century. Before that time, making sense of the market was hard. Datasets were rare and suspect. There were no useful indices and no centralized sources of prices or dividends. Instead, there was just lots of partial information, from newspapers, journals, from various brokers, from New York, and from other regional exchanges. Though the contours of the U.S. stock market were seen through these selective data, anecdotes, and media narratives, the ubiquity of dividends and their association with successful enterprises cannot be doubted. In my prior works, I've cited Groucho Marx (yes …), Karl Marx (yes …), Mark Twain, and Ulysses S. Grant, among many others, on the centrality of the dividend to a stock's attraction. For the early U.S. stock market, it is not particularly hard to see the relevance of dividends to investing. Make your way to your local library. Review its copy of *Moody's Manual of Corporation Securities*, the subsequent *Moody's Analysis of Investments*, the long-running *Commercial and Financial Chronicle (CFC)*, and others of their ilk from the late 19th and early 20th centuries. You will observe the same thing. That's not to mention the more obvious *Moody's Dividend Record*, a publication that started in 1930 and continues to this day as the *Mergent Annual Dividend Record*. Apparently, stock dividends were important enough to warrant their own publications.

In their descriptions of companies that were publicly traded and were of any size, the dividend was *sine qua non* unless the company was in trouble. Notwithstanding the centrality of a cash-based relationship between investors and large successful companies in this period, it is important to place these assertions in historical context. Notably from the perspective of today's investor is that while all major publicly traded corporations not in distress paid dividends, those cash payments differed from what we are used to seeing today. Preferred shares were far more frequently encountered than they are now. They often represented 50% or more of a company's capitalization. As the name suggests, dividends on preferred shares came first, ahead of those paid on common. And many companies had both types, preferred equity and common stock, outstanding. They would pay on the preferred and might or might not pay on the common. And they could pay at one rate on the former and a different rate on the latter. This capital structure reflected the 19th-century's boom-and-bust business cycle. By the end of the century, investors wanted a *de jure* guarantee before putting up more capital for companies, especially railroads. Even for new issues that did not have a troubled past, it was common to start the capitalization process with both preferred and common shares.

In addition, dividends were quoted quite differently. They were listed as a percent of par value of the stock. The latter was usually $100 per share. In that case, a quoted "6% dividend" would equate to $6.00 per share, often paid semi-annually, in two $3.00 increments. In other instances, the quote could be a 1.5% dividend paid quarterly ($1.50 per payment adding up to $6.00 per year). Investors considering a purchase had to do the math of the actual yield based on the purchase price. For instance, if the shares in question were then trading at $80, the actual annual yield was 7.5%; at $120 per share, the yield was 5%. Because par value of $100 was so common, it made it somewhat easier for investors to get a sense of whether a company was trading well (above $100) or not so well (below $100).

Keeping in mind those time-specific practices, you can see, for instance, in the 1901 volume of *Moody's Manual of Corporation Securities* numerous real-world examples of the centrality of the dividend to the investment equation. Early in the thick alphabetical tome, we encounter the American Bicycle Company, one of many trust-like entities created to buy up individual manufacturers in what was a crowded industry. So while the bike craze was more than a decade old (and the Sherman Antitrust Act dated from 1890), the American Bicycle Company had just been incorporated in 1899 and controlled 60% of bicycles sold in the United States and Canada at that time.

> The Capital stock of the company consists of $10,000,000 7% Cumulative Preferred stock and $20,000,000 Common Stock, all issued and outstanding. Par $100. The preferred stock has prior rights, both as to assets and 7% dividends. Up to September 1901, no dividend has been paid.

I quote this example to make the point that while not all corporations paid dividends, all were expected to unless they were new (as ABC was) or in distress.[3]

In the same *Moody's Manual*, General Electric was listed as paying a 7% semi-annual dividend on its preferred and 6% quarterly on its common, a rate that had been increased to 8% in early 1901. Then as now, a rising dividend was a good thing. Similarly recognizable, Westinghouse Electric and Manufacturing also paid differential rates on its preferred (7%) and common (most recently 1.5% per quarterly payment or 6% annually). Westinghouse had a par value of $50 which resulted in absolute dividend amounts of $3.50 and $3, respectively. All other things being equal, the Westinghouse shares would trade at about half of the GE peers. American Car & Foundry Company, Bethlehem Steel (quoted on the Philadelphia Exchange), International Paper, Rochester Optical & Camera Company (quoted on the local Rochester Exchange), National Biscuit (an ancestor of today's Nabisco), and Western Union all tell a roughly similar tale. Thousands of such narratives exist in which the ubiquity and significance of cash payments to shareholders cannot be doubted. In contrast, the American Malting Company had stopped paying its dividends in 1899. A special committee investigated the company and discovered that the "dividends had been paid when not earned, and that the Company as a whole had not been economically managed." Such is the risk of investing in the stock market. ... At that time and place, the definition of risk necessarily included the payment or non-payment of the dividend.[4]

The leading issues of the cash age could not have been more different from the cashless or nearly cashless technology giants that are at the apex of today's stock market. Railroads dominated the U.S. stock market throughout the 19th century and well into the 20th century. While indices with sector weights are not available for this early period, casual observation as well as academic studies indicates that railroads were by far the largest segment of the regularly traded market.[5] And unlike today's behemoths, these companies maintained a rigorously cash-based relationship with their owners. They had to. Railroads required capital and lots of it. For all the cash put in, investors expected cash in return. As a result, a railroad not paying its preferred dividends was a "busted road." In contrast, a railroad paying cash on its preferred and its common was a successful one. The *Commercial and Financial Chronicle*'s annual railroad supplement would open each issue by listing the trailing seven years (and later ten years) of dividends for each railroad listed. The summary tables on each page featured the last dividend paid for each road. The railroad section of *Moody's Analyses of Investments* even calculated a dividend available per mile of road. *Yes, a dividend per mile of railroad!* Moody's stock ratings at the time used a simple formula that included profit coverage of the dividend.[6] Even IPOs had dividends. You read that correctly. The Coca-Cola Company, listed in 1919, did not have enough of a record in 1920 to get a full Moody's rating, but it did have preferred shares yielding 7% and common paying $4 per year. That was a mere one year after its listing.[7]

While I prefer the feel of the hard copy found in my local Carnegie library, many of these journals and books have been digitized in recent years. A full run of the very important *CFC*, for instance, is available online courtesy of the St. Louis Federal Reserve Bank.[8] Many of the later and more detailed *Moody's Manuals* have also been digitized and are increasingly available via the internet.[9] Avail yourself of them. Choose a year, choose a company, and find a dividend, perhaps not for the mining companies, for the distressed companies, and for the pure and obvious speculations. For the rest, you will find a cash relationship between owner and asset—the ownership dividend. That should not come as a surprise. It was, is, and will again be the business norm, even in the stock market.

DIVIDENDS AND DATABASES

Due to the paucity of standardized data, empirical analyses of the pre-Crash stock market have been hard to produce. In recent decades, however, a diligent group of historically oriented finance professors, most recently Edward F. McQuarrie from Santa Clara University, has overseen a herculean effort to systematize the scattered sources for the 19th and early 20th centuries. That effort has produced a database of prices and dividends for the period before the more reliable and better-known data kicks in. In the description of the financial archeology that was involved in getting a better picture of the first stage of the U.S. stock market, it is abundantly clear that the dividends were as crucial as the share prices for the archeologists. While these new databases are still in the shadows of the data that are available from 1926 to the present, they represent a vast improvement over the prior guesswork. And review of these spreadsheets confirms the anecdotal observations, asserting the significance of dividends in understanding returns and success in the U.S. stock market. Indeed, in an aggregate view of the 19th century, a period in which stock prices were often flat for long intervals, the dividend return constituted much if not all of the total return to investors from stocks for extended periods. While that ceased being the case in what McQuarrie calls the "modern regime"—after 1926—it is still worth noting.[10] McQuarrie has made his database available for download and inspection.[11] It is possible to find zeroes in the dividend column for smaller companies or at the beginning of a run, but they are clearly the exception and give way to mid- and high single-digit figures in a few years.

Yale's Robert Shiller makes the same point in his publicly available database. It is aggregate data drawn from a variety of sources, but the point is the same: dividends mattered, with market yields between 4 and 6% and payout ratios between 50 and 70% for the period when his data begin, 1871, up until the past few decades.[12] The CRSP database of individual stocks, "takes over" in 1926. The story is the same here. Well into the postwar decades, all established companies of any significant size that were not in distress paid dividends. On a market cap-weighted basis, more than 90% of companies were payers from 1926 until the 1980s (with the exception of two economic downturns in the early 1930s and the early 1970s). The percentage of payers then fell briefly below the 70% level in the late 1990s dot-com bubble. Over the past two decades, it recovered to around 80%, only to fall again to the 70% mark in the past few years. On an equal-weighted basis, the figures are somewhat lower—more small companies did not pay dividends—but show a similar pattern.[13] The Compustat database from S&P Global Market Intelligence provides granular, company-level data starting in the early 1960s. Through the late 1970s, when the database includes 4,000 entries per year, including many smaller businesses not expected to make distributions, the dividend ratio still stays in the 60–70% range.[14] For a perspective on individual securities, *Moody's Dividend Record*—referenced earlier—chronicles the continued relevance and omnipresence of dividends from 1930 onward. Other traditional media sources, which are more easily accessible, do as well. Check out the archives of *The Wall Street Journal* (founded 1889), *Barron's* (founded 1921), etc.

THEN AND NOW

The ubiquity of dividends in all but the most recent period is not to suggest a simplistic black-and-white, dividend-no dividend, investing climate. There were numerous other important differences that could influence the nature of dividends as the measure of a company's success. For instance, the tax environment differed radically. After the introduction of the federal income tax in 1913, dividends were generally exempt from taxation for decades.[15] Starting in 1954, dividends were taxed as ordinary income, at the prevailing high rates, with a variety of initial exemptions and credits. This coincidentally and very importantly is when modern academic finance was coming into being, in the 1950s, 1960s, and 1970s. In this period, there still weren't major stocks without dividends, but the capital gains could be timed; the dividend payments could not. The academics also didn't like—with justification—the fact that dividends were taxed twice, at the corporate level as profits, and then again at the shareholder level. In short, it was a hostile environment to be a dividend investor, but there wasn't much choice. Equities paid dividends; dividends were highly taxed. Somehow it worked.

The ice broke starting with the Tax Reform Act of 1986. The top rate on personal income (and therefore on dividends and capital gains) was reduced to 28%. The rate on top earners began to creep up within a few years, but for most investors, it stayed at 28%. The new century brought lower levels of taxation on dividends and realized capital gains. And importantly, it kept the rate the same for the two forms of return. That's been the case now for the past 20 years. The 2003 tax-law changes featured the lowest rate in a century, at 15%, but starting in 2013, the rate became 23.8% for top earners. It is the same for qualified dividend income (from tax-paying corporations) and for long-term capital gains.

So when not taxed at all—the first period—dividends defined the market. When highly taxed—the second period—they were still omnipresent until the world went topsy-turvy in the 1990s. And then when they were less taxed versus the prior decades—the third period—dividends retreated substantially. There will be additional discussion of taxation later. Suffice it here to note that while taxation may be an important factor in the investment equation for many market participants, it does not appear to have been—nor should it be—a structural one in regard to the relationship between owners of companies and the companies themselves.

Breadth of ownership is a more significant difference between the historical market and what we have currently. In 1602 and for centuries after, stock ownership was a narrow matter, limited to elites and those supporting them. On the eve of the Crash in 1929, after a decade of exuberance and a whole new generation of punters jumping in, only 10% of U.S. households owned traded securities. Stocks had high visibility in the 1920s, but they were not the mainstay of middle-class retirement planning that they have become a century later. In the post-World War II period, more and more of the population gained access to retirement investment programs (such as the 401(k) programs created in 1978), brokerage accounts, and pension funds. Today, more than half of U.S. households have a stake in equities, usually indirectly through mutual funds, index funds, and ETFs.

Stock buybacks offer another telling contrast. Although securities were redeemed and retired as part of the periodic recapitalization of companies, buybacks as a supposed means of "rewarding" company owners made no sense until the most recent decades. For the first two centuries of the U.S. market, companies were raising capital, not retiring it. That stands in stark contrast to the current paradigm that treats buybacks as "normal" and similar to a dividend. They are not. As discussed in Chapter 3, they are historically anomalous and most certainly not the vaunted "returning cash to shareholders" advertised to investors. More generally, business and macroeconomic conditions were dramatically different. The railroads that dominated the second half of the 19th century were joined in the early 20th century by other capital-intensive industrial enterprises. They were strikingly unlike the service economy that has emerged over the past half-century. It is ironic and worth calling out that the capital-intensive historical market paid material dividends, and the less capital-intensive service-economy market does not.

***

I emphasize the central role of dividends in the structure of the stock market starting more than a century ago and continuing through the 1980s not because I expect a crude return to the past. There is no particular need now for every public company to have preferred shares or to quote dividends relative to the par value of shares. Dividends per mile of railroad is a fascinating measurement tool, but it is not relevant to today's investors. Those are superficial, time-specific manifestations of an underlying business relationship between investors and companies. Instead, this history tour is simply to highlight that all leading companies, and even moderately successful ones, for most of the first two centuries of the U.S. stock market (from its 1802 nominal start date) maintained a cash relationship with their investors, necessarily and logically.

While that cash relationship was the expected norm, it had not yet been made explicit. The detailed math of net present value applied to investments would come starting in the late 19th century and get worked out fully by the 1930s. But the expected standard cash relationship between company and investor in the period before the academics explained it all was a natural manifestation of centuries, if not millennia, of business ownership, particularly when that ownership took the form of minority stakes in companies about which minimal other information was available. Investors did, do, and will continue to hope for great future outcomes for their riskier investments. But in the meantime, the cash dividend (or bond coupon) was real and tangible when little else about an investment was. Investors instinctively understood, as most successful businesspeople have from time immemorial, that the value of an asset—what you might pay for it—is based on what you could expect to derive from that asset as its owner. And, echoing economist and finance pioneer Irving Fisher in 1906, even if your intention was to sell the asset a week or a month or a year later, the buyer was or should be doing the same mental and actual math: what utility—that is, the cashflow—would they derive from long-term ownership? That is simply in line with the nature of business. That would change starting in the 1990s, but investors should appreciate that long-term cash-free or very cash-light investments are anomalous, an exception to the business and historical norm.

NOTES

[1] That is the beginning that we know a lot about. The beginning we know less about is covered in William Goetzmann's magisterial *Money Changes Everything: How Finance Made Civilization Possible* (Princeton: Princeton University Press, 2016). In it, Goetzmann covers the "pre-history" of modern finance and finds antecedents if not exact forms for most financial products we know today. For an example that is both prior to VOC and based on dividends, see David le Bris, William N. Goetzmann, and Sebastien Pouget, "The Present Value Relation Over Six Centuries: The Case of the Bazacle Company," *Journal of Financial Economics*, Vol. 132, no. 1 (April 2019), 248–265. For another recent overview of early joint stock companies and exchanges, see also Norton Reamer and Jesse Downing, *Investment: A History* (New York: Columbia Business School Publishing, 2016).

[2] The Dutch East India's first cash dividend occurred in 1612, a decade after its launch. Bris et al., "The Present Value Relation over Six Centuries," confirm that the Bazacle Company's real return was essentially its average 5% dividend yield.

[3] *Moody's Manual of Corporation Securities*, Vol. 2 (1901), 614–615; Vol. 4 (1903), 1307–1309. Two years later, the company failed and restructured itself as a division of the Pope Manufacturing Company.

[4] *Moody's Manual of Corporation Securities*, Vol. 2 (1901), 627–630, 636–637, 661–666, 674–675, 836–839, 854, 977, 985–987, 1055–1057.

[5] Edward F. McQuarrie, "Introducing a New Database of 19th Century Railroads Before Cowles and Macaulay," SSRN 3011486 (2021), Table 1, 41. Also anecdotally indicated at www.library.hbs.edu/hc/railroads/finance.html and referenced in Elroy Dimson, Paul Marsh, and Mike Staunton, *Triumph of the Optimists: 101 Years of Global Investment Returns* (Princeton: Princeton University Press, 2002). Banks and insurance companies were not traded on the NYSE until well into the 20th century.

[6] *Financial Review*, Railroad Supplement, volumes reviewed from 1893 to 1914. *Moody's Analyses of Investment*, Vol. 10 (1919), Part I, Railroads, for the Chicago, Indianapolis & Louisville Railroad, 172–178. For the stock rating, see *Moody's Analysis of Investments*, Vol. 9 (1918), Part II, Public Utilities & Industrials, for the El Paso Electric Company, 275 & Liggett & Myers Tobacco Company, 737.

[7] *Moody's Analyses of Investments*, Vol. 11 (1920), Part II, 1358.

[8] https://fraser.stlouisfed.org/title?browse=C#1339.

[9] For instance, www.libraries.rutgers.edu/databases/mergent_archives.

[10] McQuarrie: "Stocks for the Long Run? Sometimes Yes, Sometimes No.," SSRN 3805927 (2021), his earlier "Introducing a New Database of 19th Century Railroads Before Cowles & Macaulay," SSRN 3011486 (2021), and his "New Bank and Transportation Stock Indexes from 1793 to 1871, with Comparisons across Region and Sector, and Against Prior Indexes," SSRN 3480838 (2021).

[11] www.edwardfmcquarrie.com/?p=579.

[12] The S&P 500 Index was formally launched in 1957. Shiller uses its precursors to take his data back to 1871. The home page of Professor Robert Shiller: http://econ.yale.edu/~shiller/.

[13] Largest 90% of companies in the CRSP U.S. stock database, as ranked by market capitalization annually. ©2022 Center for Research in Security Prices, LLC, An affiliate of the University of Chicago School of Business.

[14] S&P Global Market Intelligence and FactSet, 2023.

[15] With a brief, four-year exception in the late 1930s.

2

FALLACY OR PHILOSOPHY
ACADEMIC FINANCE'S BIG, 60-YEAR WAR ON DIVIDENDS

How did we get to the current state of affairs where investment in successful companies based on current and future distributable cashflows occupies just a tiny corner of the U.S. marketplace for stocks? That is from the investor's perspective. From the corporate perspective, the questions are why major businesses with ample internal cashflows do not reward shareholders in cash and why they are not called out for it. It is a strange world indeed. The movement away from a cash-based ownership relationship occurred in parallel in the halls of academe and on the floor of the stock exchange. This chapter focuses on the professors.

THE DIVIDEND PUZZLE

It is an article of faith in academic finance that the proper value of a project or an investment is associated with the net present value of the discounted future cashflows of said project or investment.

DOI: 10.4324/9781003292272-3

This approach graces most written valuation work, from a passing reference early in academic finance articles to the obligatory cashflow model at the end of stock-analyst reports. It is reflected in the acronyms of the trade: DDM, IRR, DCF, and NPV.[1] Paths diverge as to the best form—is it just cashflows to equity, is it distributed cash payments to the equity holders, is it levered or unlevered, the terminal value approach, etc.? And there is a vast array of calculation options. Although this framework has been largely ignored for the past few decades in the stock market's "anything-goes" environment, it still constitutes the agreed-upon general philosophical framework for business valuation.

This consensus on valuing companies based on cashflows creates a striking paradox, one that is at the center of this work. For the past 60-some years, the leading lights of academic finance have been nearly equally united in their explicit rejection of the most straightforward, "default" manifestation of a discounted cashflow approach for minority shareholders of publicly traded equities. That is, they dismiss the dividend, the income stream reserved for the lowly, none-too-bright retail investors, for widows and orphans, and other lesser souls. I'm not suggesting that the entire finance community shares this view. There is a dedicated resistance, covered later in this account. But as far as academic views that make it from gown to town, that are broadly disseminated and recognized in the practitioner community, yes, it is the consensus to be dismissive of companies paying dividends and for investors to seek them out.

In this context, academic finance has been faced with an extended whodunnit, a "puzzle" as Fischer Black characterized dividend payments in 1976. And it wasn't just a minor puzzle. In a much-quoted line from 1983, one of the field's leading investigators wrote that "the nearly universal policy of paying substantial dividends is the primary puzzle in the economics of corporate finance."[2] Those comments were made when most companies still paid a substantial dividend.

More than 40 years after these comments were made, the real puzzle is not why dividends are paid and sought after, as the academics questioned, but why anyone would think otherwise. As is often the case in my analysis, the answer is substantially historical. That is, it is all too common in finance and investing to assume that the "rules" are the rules, have always been that way, and will always be that way. Memorize the rules and make a lot of money. Well, it turns out that is not correct. Many of the so-called rules by which we invest (or live) have a specific context of creation that explains them. They were relevant in that context. They may or may not be relevant in a different context. Or as John Maynard Keynes supposedly but apparently never said, "When the facts change, I alter my conclusions. What do you do?" In a prior work, I took the same approach to Modern Portfolio Theory.[3] I pointed out its historical context, asserted that the facts had changed, and encouraged investors to consider whether it is time for a new port-folio construction framework. The academic disdain for dividend investing falls into the same category. It has a history; I am sharing that history. You can judge whether it is still relevant.

EARLY UNDERSTANDING

Let's begin with crucial context. With notable exceptions such as the Dutch East India Company and its English equivalent a cen-tury later, the early publicly traded businesses up until the mid-to late 19th century tended to be small, focused, and local. They were bigger than a family business but not hugely complicated and diverse. And their ownership was similarly narrow and limited. The separation of ownership and management existed, but that gap was not yet what it would become. In the late 19th and early 20th centuries, that changed. Businesses became much bigger and much more complicated. Think Standard Oil, U.S. Steel, the Pennsylvania Railroad, etc. As they grew in size and complexity, the traditional management and cashflow linkage between owner and operator became even more attenuated than what it had been in the early iterations of the joint stock company. Now there were larger boards, layers of managers, lots of employees, and many smaller, unrelated investors.

It took a while for the academy to catch up with these new businesses and their innovative structures. To be fair, this is partly because the finance wing of the academy didn't exist at that time. Business schools are an early 20th-century phenomenon. Finance, as a discipline separate from economics, came even later. The systematic study of these new forms didn't occur until about a half-century after their broad appearance and domination of the business landscape. An early effort that made a big splash was *The Modern Corporation and Private Property*, published in 1932 by Adolf Berle—an attorney, Roosevelt buddy, and law school professor—and Gardiner Means, an economist. The two professors were not thrilled about the direction of modern capitalism—specifically the separation of owners and operators, but that is a topic for another day. It is my argument here that, given that most shareholders of the new large entities were now minority investors with little direct control over the enterprise, they should focus quite intensely and necessarily on the distributable cashflows that they would receive from their contributed capital.

At almost the exact same time, investor and Columbia Business School professor Benjamin Graham wrote the first modern comprehensive account of stock market investing, *Security Analysis*. It came out in 1934. Please read it. It's all about dividends. Graham may well come closest to the simple assertion that the purpose of the modern corporation is to aggregate capital, build scale businesses, generate profits, and distribute them to company owners. Everyone regards him as the father of "value" investing, but I would strongly encourage you to go back and read his original work to appreciate how much that value was tied up with a company's distributable profits. (Use the original 1934 edition.) A few years later, in 1938, John Burr Williams, a former stock analyst and investor who had gone back to school to get a Ph.D., published his dissertation, *The Theory of Investment Value*. It worked out in great detail for the first time the main math of discounted cashflow valuations and dividend discount models applied to stocks. (Yale Professor Irving Fisher had outlined the logic in 1906 in his *The Nature of Capital and Income*.) Along the way, a host of practitioners and a handful of additional academics have highlighted the benefits of approaching stocks from the perspective of dividends received. In short, owning businesses for their dividends has more than four centuries of practical history behind it, and at least the first half of the 20th century of academics working out the math and putting it in print.

Prominent business leaders at the time understood, even without a blessing from the academy, that dividends were the appropriate form of return for investors providing capital. The chief of General Motors made it clear in a 1935 interview in the *New York Times* that GM's dividend policy would be based on the company's profitability and its future investment needs. Alfred Sloan concluded his piece with the statement that "[t]he most important point I want to make is that General Motors stockholders can rely upon the directors to pass on the largest possible share of the earnings consistent with the needs of the business."[4] Sloan's approach might be considered a given for a successful enterprise now, but to the extent that these widely held, large, publicly traded corporations were still relatively new in the early 20th century, dividend policy required explanation. My point is that a company that dominated an industry for over a half-century felt completely comfortable paying robust dividends while investing in its business.

So before the academics bolted in the second half of the 20th century, grounding valuation exercises in discounted cashflows, and by extension dividend payments, from publicly traded companies to minority shareholders, was established as the *narrated, explicit cornerstone of valuation work*. As of the mid-1930s, the ability to pay and increase dividends over time remained the key measure of a successful publicly traded business. Early academic finance was in agreement with this notion. There was no puzzle as to why companies would pay dividends and why investors would want them. Now to be fair, dividends were not taxed at all in the period, with the exception of 1936–1939. So their payment and receipt did not have the marginal disadvantage that they would have from 1954 to 1985. Similarly, the only stocks without dividends were those that couldn't afford to pay them, clearly speculative or start-up or failing ventures.

From this perspective, dividend payments were understood to be consistent with the broader idea of business ownership beyond stock holdings. An investor might purchase a minority stake in any business and expect to receive a proportional share of the profits in return. It's not at all complicated and, to a great extent, the work done by the individuals referenced earlier was just codifying centuries of actual commerce and investment practice where a stream of future payments would be equated in some fashion or another to the market value of an asset. Just think of any reasonably thought-through, unforced purchase of productive agricultural land at any time in recorded history. The exercise becomes more developed over the centuries until it is formally articulated in the early 20th century.

While the term dividend has rightly and accurately passed into general usage with a positive connotation—as in an activity that pays a dividend—the term "return" has evolved over time. It started out signifying the physical return of cash at the end of an investment—the handing over of the initial investment amount, with some extra to represent the profit. That was the nature of the earliest joint-stock companies associated with specific ventures, such as bringing spices, silks, and other rarities by boat to Europe from Asia. It was a liquidating payment. Over time, it came to represent the cash payment of profits in cash from an ongoing enterprise. Or if from a private asset, the returns were the rents from real estate or the yields of the productive land. Yes, the price of an asset rose and fell every day on London's Exchange Alley, New York's Wall Street, and anywhere else investments were bought and sold, but non-speculative thinking about such investments, to the extent that there was such thinking, came from contemplating the income stream associated with the asset.[5] To that point, the embryonic stage of what we now call shareholder activism or good governance was about getting more dividends for shareholders. The leader of the movement, Lewis Gilbert, who was active from the 1930s to the 1980s, believed that "more corporate democracy means more corporate dividends. The reforms advocated by the movement of independent public shareholders are a matter of dollars and cents for the investor."[6]

The math of total return incorporating both price change and income generation became more formalized in the post-World War II period as datasets, indices, and total return calculation mechanisms appeared. Starting in the 1950s, Modern Portfolio Theory (MPT) emerged as an approach that, while necessarily including the dividend in the total return equation, began focusing more attention on the ever-changing array of daily asset prices and their relationship to one another. As argued in my *Getting Back to Business* from 2018, MPT is a theory for people focusing on datasets of prices, not a theory of business ownership through the stock market. That is, over the past 70 years, the term "return" has evolved from a definite and expected cash payment to a mostly non-cash return, the change in the publicly quoted price of an asset. There's nothing per se wrong with that, but it's important to point out the history of these concepts. This sustained shift in perspective—from ownership of an income-producing asset to asset-price maximization with little attention paid to the income stream—creates one of the foundations for the paradigm of the past several decades.

DIVIDEND "IRRELEVANCE"

The intellectual history of this movement away from dividends is well known. It is, in fact, so well known that I believe many investors simply cite the founding document (from 1961) but don't actually read it or haven't read since their schooldays. That document is worth reviewing closely.[7] A small portion of it remains relevant. The rest of it is so woefully out-of-date as to now meet the standard of being wrong. The long-deceased authors received Nobel Prizes for their efforts and have privileged positions in the pantheon of academic finance. Merely suggesting that this particular work might no longer be relevant will invite ridicule from the academy. But as Keynes famously warned at the end of *The General Theory* (1936),

> the ideas of economists and political philosophers, both when they are right and when they are wrong, are more powerful than is commonly understood. Indeed the world is ruled by little else. Practical men, who believe themselves to be quite exempt from any intellectual influences, are usually the slaves of some defunct economist.

In 1958, Franco Modigliani and Merton Miller (popularly known as M&M) made what was then and still is now a common-sense argument that the value of a firm should be based on its assets and earnings potential, not how the entity's balance sheet is financed. It was a whiteboard argument, but it put forth the important conceptual framework that the capital structure of a firm should—all other things (including taxes) being kept equal—be irrelevant to the market value of a business. Three years later, in the *Journal of Business*, M&M extended their argument from the front end of the horse—a company's capital structure—to the business end, the company's distributions and returns. Consistent with the increasing focus on share prices, they asked "is there an optimum [dividend] payout ratio or range of ratios that maximizes the current worth of the shares?"[8] That is, does a higher payout ratio lead to higher share prices? The very formulation of the question highlights the importance of dividends in driving share prices at the time. (Many current stock market investors would struggle even to understand the question.)

Their subsequent argument is redolent with the rational actor and perfect markets theories popular at the time, but the key assertion is that "the higher the dividend payout in any period, the more new capital that must be raised from external sources to maintain any desired level of investment."[9] M&M therefore concluded that a company's dividend policy is irrelevant because higher payouts necessarily lead to dilutive capital raising for a given level of capital expenditure by the company. Lower payouts lead to less dilutive capital raised for the same level of investment. The two different approaches to the challenge of growth result in the same outcome at the individual share level. Hence, a company's dividend payout policy should be irrelevant to the price of a share. Their conclusion creates a rather elegant symmetry of irrelevance involving the capital structure going in, and the distributions coming out.

CAPITAL INTENSITY THEN AND NOW

Did you catch the mistake? It is hiding there in plain sight. Hint: in 1961, it wasn't a mistake, but it is a huge one today and one that more or less reverses the authors' conclusions for today's corporate managers and investors. The key phrase is "for a given level of investment." And you will note the critical assumption that the spending involved is invariably greater than the company's available cashflow. Thus, it requires external capital, more if the payout ratio is higher, less if the payout ratio is lower. That's the rub. Using the simplest definition of free cashflow (FCF)—Net Income plus Depreciation minus Capital Expenditures—for companies in the Compustat database from the early 1960s, we can see in Table 2.1 that the United States was still in its industrial and manufacturing heyday. At that time, the country's 500 leading companies had substantial growth opportunities to pursue, and those programs were capital intensive. All that Plant Property and Equipment came at a cash cost. For the five years from 1962 through 1966, FCF after dividend payments was consistently negative due to very high capital expenditures. Capex to sales ranged from 9% to 12%. The dividend payout ratio ranged from 67% to 74%. In this context, the leading companies of the day were free cashflow negative and would need external capital to fund all of their investment plans and pay their dividend. In that case, M&M made sense. Fast forward 60 years, however, and M&M's base case is no longer remotely the case. At the aggregate level, the top 500 companies for the period from 2015 through 2019 (and 2022, skipping the two pandemic years) were highly FCF positive, with much lower capital intensity, in the 6% range.

It is true that a small subset of the market remains in M&M territory. Utilities now represent just 3.18% of the S&P 500 Index (as of 12/31/22). They do regularly run FCF negative and have to raise external capital to modernize our power grid. Many Real Estate Investment Trusts (REITs) fall into the same category. They are another 2.71% of the S&P 500 Index. In theory, and holding all other factors equal, M&M still applies to them. It might also pertain to certain capital-intensive companies with dividend payments structurally and regularly in excess of their cashflows from operations minus capital expenditures. So how much of the market does the M&M dividend irrelevancy proposition apply to now? On an ongoing basis, is it perhaps 10% of the S&P 500

Table 2.1 Top 500 U.S. Companies by Market Capitalization in the Compustat North America Database

Values in Millions USD	1962	1963	1964	1965	1966	2015	2016	2017	2018	2019	2022
Net Income	17,227	19,342	23,238	26,479	29,615	889,921	936,887	1,055,215	1,210,613	1,296,711	1,532,532
Depreciation	11,753	12,624	14,948	16,313	18,701	573,078	598,283	638,216	667,221	706,963	761,140
Capex	18,921	19,915	26,173	31,454	36,051	695,485	680,472	680,268	766,611	767,594	896,128
Free Cashflow	10,059	12,051	12,012	11,338	12,265	767,513	854,698	1,013,163	1,111,223	1,236,081	1,397,544
Dividends	13,665	14,455	16,373	17,759	19,349	410,089	429,525	446,610	489,256	522,760	613,427
Payout Ratio	79.3%	74.7%	70.5%	67.1%	65.3%	46.1%	45.8%	42.3%	40.4%	40.3%	40.0%
Post Dividend-Free Cashflow	(3,606)	(2,404)	(4,361)	(6,421)	(7,084)	357,424	425,173	566,553	621,966	713,321	784,117
Sales	252,765	273,759	307,864	340,930	387,645	10,752,801	10,823,291	11,449,989	12,213,879	12,838,548	15,573,097
Capex to Sales	7.5%	7.3%	8.5%	9.2%	9.3%	6.5%	6.3%	5.9%	6.3%	6.0%	5.8%
Ave. Div. Yield	6.38%	5.08%	5.29%	5.05%	6.01%	2.09%	1.99%	1.75%	2.20%	1.89%	2.13%
Median Div. Yield	3.24%	2.94%	2.80%	2.83%	3.35%	1.81%	1.75%	1.52%	1.90%	1.61%	1.48%
Div. Paying Count	482	482	482	481	480	396	397	393	390	381	373
Total Count	500	500	500	500	500	500	500	500	500	500	500
Ratio	96.4%	96.4%	96.4%	96.2%	96.0%	79.2%	79.4%	78.6%	78.0%	76.2%	74.6%

Source: S&P Global Market Intelligence; FactSet, 2023.

Note: Drawn from all U.S. common stocks in Compustat North America Database with Market Cap. > 0, excludes ADRs and secondary listings.

Index? It can't be much more. We are now a service economy in which the overwhelming majority of S&P 500 Index companies can fund their growth plans without raising external capital. They thereby fall outside the M&M dividend irrelevancy framework. At the aggregate level, the top 500 companies in the U.S. market have been in that state since the early 1990s, with only 2001 and 2008—periods of crisis—as exceptions.[10]

INTERNALLY FINANCED COMPANIES AS A SPECIAL CASE

In their original argument, M&M presciently acknowledged a scenario in which they would be wrong: they admitted that for internally financed companies—which they call an "extreme" or "special" case—"dividend policy is indistinguishable from investment policy; and there is an optimal investment policy which does in general depend on the rate of return." M&M do not like the analytical implications of this scenario at all. They go so far as to call it "treacherous."[11] What was once dismissed with some degree of contempt now applies to the vast majority of the stock market landscape.

It is worth noting that companies repurchasing their own shares were not a prominent feature of the stock market at the time so it is not surprising that the authors did not integrate buybacks into their analysis. Since the 1990s, however, buybacks have come to dominate the stock market landscape and have regularly exceeded the S&P 500 Index aggregate dollar amount of dividends for the past two decades (with a few short-lived exceptions). When buybacks are financed from debt, the original 1958 M&M propositions would apply, as buybacks simply represent a recapitalizing of a company with a different mix of debt and equity. If the share repurchases are financed from retained earnings, then we have the same flaw that the original 1961 M&M propositions have: the dividend or buyback policy counts as an alternative to an investment decision. It may be good, bad, or neutral, but it cannot be irrelevant.

It is critically important to step back from the details and acknowledge the difference between what M&M wrote 60 years ago and how their article is used by market participants a half-century later. For sure, the article is not read. Outside of the academy, I am willing to bet that no more than 5% of market participants or investment practitioners who reference M&M or dividend irrelevancy have actually read the article or, more importantly, considered its implications in the economy and market as it is now, not in 1961. Instead, M&M is just code for the general dismissal of dividend payments by corporations—often in favor of share buybacks—and the general dismissal of cash-paying business ownership by stock investors in favor of finding the next Nasdaq darling. Note that M&M didn't say that dividends were irrelevant; they said, under their extremely narrow conditions, that dividend payout ratios should be irrelevant to the overall value of the firm. That is a specific finance claim, not a generalized disregard for dividend payments. It is not what M&M said; it's what people now think they said. There's a big difference.

That might not have been the case but for their coining of an admittedly catchy phrase—dividend irrelevancy—which goes well beyond M&M's core and quite legitimate point about external financing and dilution. Without that moniker, I suspect few market participants would recognize the original M&M dividend propositions at all. Because the dividend irrelevancy theorem is well named, it has enjoyed a longer and broader life than it should have. Don't get me wrong; M&M 1961 is not technically wrong, especially in the very narrow way that it was postulated, but it is substantially, misleadingly out of date.

CAPITAL GAINS VERSUS DIVIDENDS

That is not the main flaw, however, of M&M's dividend irrelevancy theorem. The real issue is never raised in the article or much of the academic narrative against dividend payments that I review here. That real flaw is equating capital gains to a dividend payment. Mathematically they are identical. That's the view from academic finance. Money is fungible, particularly in academic exercises involving "perfect" markets. In M&M 1961, the authors treat the matter casually: "investors always prefer more wealth to less and are indifferent as to whether a given increment to their wealth takes the form of cash payments or an increase in the market value of their holdings of shares."[12] Almost all subsequent writing on the topic agrees with that assertion, either explicitly or implicitly by trying to prove which approach leads to a greater total return. And it is true that the official and proper calculation of total return includes both and treats them equally. Moreover, the University of Chicago finance professors, your MBA program, your CFA charter—all these august sources of financial wisdom treat a dividend and a capital gain of the same nominal value as exactly equivalent.

From a business ownership perspective, however, they are not the same. They are not even close. The logic of business ownership, particularly for minority shareholders of large publicly traded companies, makes a cash distribution from profits—not going into the marketplace to harvest potential capital gains—the natural mechanism for sharing in the success of an enterprise. It is a matter of philosophy, not mathematics. To suggest otherwise is to compare 2+2 with $(18*325)*(2\wedge2)/((SQRT(400))*15)-((3\wedge3)*2)-20$ (in Excel format). Yes, both formulas equate to 4. But how you get to one is very different from how you get to the other. The former is a natural consequence of business ownership, of receiving a share of company profits after other investment needs of the business have been met. Your effort is more metaphorical than real: it involves being ready to receive "the check in the mail."

The latter is far more complicated. It involves having an unrealized capital gain at a certain time, determining that it is sufficient or necessary to meet your income needs, then going out into the marketplace, when it is open and when it is in a good mood, finding a buyer at your price (a limit order) or an acceptable price (a market order), having the trade settle without issue, and the funds making their way into your account. Instead of business ownership, it is the active diminution of your stake in the enterprise. Moreover, there are risks along the way at each step of that sequence. Individually, they may be quite small, but they are there. The biggest risk is the most obvious: having a substantial capital gain to harvest. Yes, most stocks over time gain in value, but that is a grand exercise in survivorship bias. Plenty of the data points fail and fall out. In recent decades, market sentiment has become so detached from fundamentals that one can make or lose a great deal of money in the market's playthings such as Peloton, Trupanion, etc. The enormous volatility of their share prices makes it impossible to count on any reliable, predictable harvesting of capital gains. And they also run the risk of extreme capital loss at the first sign of genuine risk on the horizon.

Hard-earned gains or losses exemplify the philosophical difference between benefitting from the ongoing ownership of an asset through receipt of a profit-sharing check versus going out into the marketplace to raise cash by selling the asset. It is true that companies can cut their dividends or cease paying them altogether. So there is no such thing as a risk-free dividend stream, but in a diversified portfolio context, such events are rare and not likely to impair the investor's overall income stream.

Moreover, in a price-focused view of the world underpinning the world of capital gains, the only way to realize any actual value—real cash—from an investment is to sell a portion of it on the market. The cash value of your zero-dividend stock holding is really nothing—zero—until you sell it to someone else and settle. What a strange definition of success, where you have to part with an asset to realize its value, because it generates no return on its own? But that's what a share price is; it's just a number. You can't pay for a meal with it; you can't make a mortgage payment with it. It may make you feel good to see a higher number than yesterday, but that does not on its own allow you to increase consumption or spending. In that regard, share prices are like pieces of jewelry. They may look good on you and you may be happy about owning them, but that's where their utility ends unless you are prepared to part with the asset.

My argument has its limits. In recent decades, retirees have not been clipping equity coupons as their parents or grandparents did to meet their consumption needs. They have been taking capital gains from their many winnings. With the steadily rising market in both nominal and real terms, that's been a good strategy. So bully for harvested gains. And in fact, selling shares in retirement to slowly liquidate one's assets makes a great deal of sense. At the age of 90 years, you don't really want to own much of anything or have to think like a business owner. But markets can and do go down. For the retiree seeking a regular income stream, the sequence of their returns is critical. Any interruption in those harvested capital gains—by a big downdraft of the market—can create huge difficulties for the retiree and is a far cry from collecting a regularly scheduled dividend. I must, of course, acknowledge the modest relative taxation benefit of harvesting capital gains as opposed to collecting dividend payments in taxable accounts. Yes, capital gains taxation can be deferred or timed in a way that dividend payments cannot. But even here, there are caveats. Within a 401k and a traditional IRA, neither capital gains nor dividend income is taxed. Instead, all distributions from those accounts are taxed as ordinary income.

For many investors, those details may matter, but over the long term, they are minimal compared to the profound philosophical differences between a dividend and harvested capital gain. There are also plenty of real-world ones, such as trading costs, market conditions, and differential tax circumstances, that may make a dividend or a harvested capital gain more or less preferable than the other for individual and institutional investors.

Whether in theory or in practice, these two activities—on the one hand, clipping your coupons; on the other hand, going out and selling securities—are most certainly not the same. Having capital gains depends on market sentiment, on the views of people often far removed from the activities of a company. In contrast, dividends are a function of a company's operations. A dollar may be fungible; how it is generated is not. Drawing this distinction—between a capital markets activity and a business outcome—may be the most important assertion in this book. The rest of the argument follows naturally from it.

INDIFFERENCE BECOMES DISAPPEARANCE

This philosophical difference between the two forms of return came to light 15 years after M&M when, in 1976, MIT Professor Fischer Black pondered why dividends existed at all.[13] In a brief essay in the *Journal of Portfolio Management*, Black admitted to being unable to figure out why companies paid dividends or why investors sought them out. It was for him "a puzzle, with pieces that just don't fit together." His main argument concerns taxes. At that time, they were higher on dividends than on capital gains. The former could not be timed; the latter could. And from a corporate tax perspective, dividend payments are not deductible, unlike interest payments on bonds. As a result, dividends were subject to double taxation, first at the corporate level and then at the investor level. Black sums up the problem: "With taxes, investors and corporations are no longer indifferent to the level of dividends. They prefer smaller dividends or no dividends at all."

Black finds pro-dividend arguments about transaction costs for harvesting capital gains to be unconvincing. He similarly dismisses the idea that dividends are useful as a management signaling tool. He explores other potential reasons for dividend payments, such as trustee bias, pressure from retail investors, etc. None persuades him. Like M&M, Black acknowledges that companies with investment programs less than their free cashflow—he uses different words—might have reason to pay a dividend. And like M&M 15 years earlier, Black considers these "special cases" that are "relatively rare." Let me repeat: those rare instances are now the clear and overwhelming majority of cases. Fourteen years later in 1990, Black, then at Goldman Sachs, reiterated his view in a brief statement in the *Financial Analysts Journal*.[14] With a flourish, he ended by forecasting that "taxable [dividends] will gradually vanish." *Nota bene*: 30 years after that assertion, 45 years after his original statement and 60 after M&M, investors and companies continue to defy the academics. Vive la résistance.

Black's line of thought came to dominate the academic narrative about, or shall we say against, dividend payments. Assistant professor after assistant professor have tried to figure out the puzzle. The ever-thoughtful and even-handed financial journalist Peter Bernstein penned an argument in 1996 titled simply, "The Puzzle."[15] A very sympathetic bridge between practitioner town and academic gown, Bernstein approached the challenge from the perspective of returns. By the mid-1990s, dividend payouts and yields were down and the stock market was booming. If dividends mattered to investors, he reasoned, this would be a headscratcher, and troubling for future returns. He concludes, however, that low yields do not presage low future returns. In effect, dividends no longer matter. Along the way, he acknowledges the role that dividends have and can play in the investment equation, including those reflecting the basic tenet of business ownership, a means for investors to control management somewhat, a mechanism for the investor to guide consumption, etc. In the end, however, Bernstein, like Black, dismisses these arguments as unpersuasive with investors. And he sides with academic finance in writing that "money is money, whether we dress it up in the costume of income or the costume of principal." Bernstein finishes as Black does, without an answer to the puzzle.

And the hostility remains. In preparing this text, I came upon perhaps the most concise summary (from 2003) of the academic argument against dividends: it is that "the economic consequence of dividends is an involuntarily tax liability to the owners of the firm imposed on a marginal liquidation of their ownership."[16] That is, a dividend represents both an unnecessary tax bill and a smaller stake in the company resulting from the company being forced to hand out cash. It is hard to come up with a more damning description. It goes beyond just the genuine challenge of taxation to one of actual business ownerships that by receiving one's share of the profits, not leaving them in the corporation, one is participating in the forced diminution of the enterprise.

IT'S BEHAVIORAL!

The academy's argument against dividends has evolved over the years. In recent decades, the initial orthodox finance approach, where the tax differential loomed large, has given way to a behavioral finance framework. In addition to generating tremendous insights into human behavior, behavioral finance has yielded a lot of new material on why investors might seek dividends and the problems associated with that pursuit. But in many ways, the behavioral finance take on dividend investing is just the other side of the coin to the prior approach. Rather than assuming investors are consistently rational and all-knowing (and avoid dividends for the then-relevant tax reasons), the behavioralists highlight "the thousand natural shocks that flesh is heir to" when it comes to investing. For a full list of those shocks, see the works of Kahneman & Tversky, Richard Thaler, and Meir Statman,[17] among many others. Instead of being perfect at decision-making, it turns out that we are often biased, which makes us rather bad at it.

While, in the orthodox approach, dividend investing is simply a "mistake" by investors who should focus on less-taxed capital gains, in the behavioral version, it is more mental: it is a "fallacy," a deficiency that is typical of investors who have biases, are not all-knowing, and make a myriad of poor judgments, in this case, about dividends. Investors are not the rational machines from the prior model. Search in the SSRN or JSTOR article catalogs and you will find a lot of academics mulling over the "dividend puzzle" from a behavioral finance perspective.

The behavioralist finance literature on dividends is now itself more than 30 years old, but it has recently been well summarized and updated by two up-and-coming scholars, Samuel M. Hartzmark and David H. Solomon. Their "Dividend Disconnect" was published in the prestigious *Journal of Finance* in 2019.[18] I had the pleasure of interviewing David Solomon for my podcast in 2020. He provided a great summary of their work in behavioral finance. In their most prominent article, they start with the obligatory reference to M&M and the philosophical assertion that a dividend is no different from a capital gain. From that premise, they pursue what they call the "disconnect" between how investors treat the income stream of an asset with the price of the asset. Having separate mental accounts, investors (supposedly) believe that their dividends are "free"—and they are (supposedly) unaware that dividends are coming out of the asset price. Since so much of the investment world is now measured and operates according to price change, not total return, the impact that dividend payments have on price returns necessarily leads to all sorts of investing and consumption distortions. They document those distortions in great detail. And they conclude that investors are "more naïve ... [in regard to dividends] than academic finance has generally assumed." Of course, I beg to differ. It is less a matter of naivete than the very real difference between academic theory, on one hand, and business and investment practice, on the other.

***

The academy's debate about dividends has gone on for decades—under high tax regimes, under varying tax regimes, under low and equal tax regimes. During those decades it has alternately assumed rational, all-knowing investors, and punters who make mistake after mistake. Regardless of the environment, the leading schools of thought – the classical finance community decades ago and more recently the behavioral finance camp—have looked unkindly at investing for dividends. Try as they might, the most visible and audible finance professors cannot find their way to the most natural and logical form of rewarding minority-stake investors in publicly traded firms.

NOTES

[1] Dividend Discount Model (DDM), Internal Rate of Return (IRR), Discounted Cash Flow (DCF), Net Present Value (NPV).

[2] Martin S. Feldstein and Jerry Green, "Why Do Companies Pay Dividends?" *The American Economic Review*, Vol. 73, no. 1 (March 1983), 17–30. The quote opens the article.

[3] Daniel Peris, *Getting Back to Business* (New York: McGraw-Hill, 2018).

[4] "Sloan Explains Dividend Policy," *New York Times*, September 12, 1935.

[5] The full history of businesses paying dividends to company owners remains to be written, but you can catch glimpses of it in George M. Frankfurter and Bob G. Wood, Jr., with James Wansley, *Dividend Policy: Theory and Practice* (San Diego: Academic Press, 2003). The authors have a quite jaundiced view to the payment of dividends, but they provide a good jumping off point.

[6] Lewis D. Gilbert, *Dividends and Democracy* (Larchmont, NY: American Research Council, 1956), 3.

[7] For an earlier, initial critique, see Peris, *Getting Back to Business*, 129–140.

[8] Merton H. Miller and Franco Modigliani, "Dividend Policy, Growth, and the Valuation of Shares," *The Journal of Business*, Vol. 34, no. 4 (October 1961), 411–443; quote from 411. Hereafter referenced as M&M (1961).

[9] M&M (1961), 413.

[10] Largest 500 companies by market capitalization: Net Income + Depreciation—Capital Expenditures—Dividend Payments. Source: S&P Global Market Intelligence; FactSet, 2023.

[11] M&M (1961), 423, 424.

[12] M&M (1961), 412.

[13] Fischer Black, "The Dividend Puzzle," *The Journal of Portfolio Management*, Vol. 2, no. 2 (Winter 1976), 5–8. Updated through the late 1980s by Steven V. Mann, "The Dividend Puzzle: A Progress Report," *Quarterly Journal of Business and Economics*, Vol. 28, no. 3 (Summer 1989), 3–35.

[14] Fischer Black, "Why Firms Pay Dividends," *Financial Analyst Journal*, Vol. 46, no. 3 (May–June 1990), 5.

[15] Peter L. Bernstein, "Dividends: The Puzzle," *Journal of Applied Corporate Finance*, Vol. 9, no. 1 (Spring 1996), 16–22.

[16] Frankfurter and Wood, with Wansley, *Dividend Policy*, 3.

[17] Daniel Kahneman and Amos Tversky, "Prospect Theory: An Analysis of Decision under Risk," *Econometrica*, Vol. 47, no. 2 (1979), 263–291; Daniel Kahneman, *Thinking Fast and Slow* (New York: Farrar, Straus, & Giroux, 2011); Richard H. Thaler, *Misbehaving: The Making of Behavioral Economics* (New York: W. W. Norton & Company, 2015); Meir Statman, *Finance for Normal People* (New York: Oxford University Press, 2017).

[18] Samuel M. Hartzmark and David H. Solomon, "The Dividend Disconnect," *The Journal of Finance*, Vol. 74, no. 5 (October 2019), 2153–2199.

3

THE CHANGING ENVIRONMENT FOR BUSINESS OWNERSHIP IN THE U.S. STOCK MARKET

The academics set the stage for the dramatic transformation of ownership in the U.S. stock market, but the professors did not make it happen. The market structure changed for different, more profound reasons. While many academic observers and more than a few practitioners have observed the diminishment of the cash relationship, there is little if any formal literature on this topic. This chapter outlines what I consider the three primary drivers of the change. The first and most important is the persistent drop in interest rates that began in 1981 and continued until late 2020. The importance of that trend on the nature of stock ownership cannot be overstated. The second is the seemingly innocuous and minor securities law change in 1982 that permitted widespread share buybacks. In terms of unexpected and unintended consequences for the market, it was the proverbial butterfly flapping its wings and a storm occurring on the other side of the planet. The third is the rise and indisputable success of Silicon Valley, an engine of world-changing innovation and capital allocation. The tax reason, so decisively promoted and purported by the academics over many

DOI: 10.4324/9781003292272-4

decades, does not figure in this process, as the tax differential is now much less than it was when dividends were more prominent.

DISAPPEARING DIVIDENDS

Correlation does not mean causation, and it is impossible to prove beyond a doubt that the shift in the market's structure is due to these causes in this order. But the logic is clear enough, and the duration of the correlation—some 40 years—is highly suggestive. But let's start with the outcome first. Dividends have been pushed into the background of the market and have disappeared entirely from parts of the landscape. That can be shown clearly using a variety of sources. The first and easiest is the aggregate market data from Robert Shiller's public database, referenced earlier, shown in Figure 3.1. There is a notable decline during the go-go years of the 1950s and 1960s, but the structural step down in both yield and payout ratio to the current level occurs later, in the 1990s.

More granular is the company-specific data from Compustat, available from 1962 to the present. Figure 3.2 clearly depicts the drop in the number of dividend payers as a percent of overall stocks to the 30% level in recent decades. That is, indeed, a sea change in market structure.

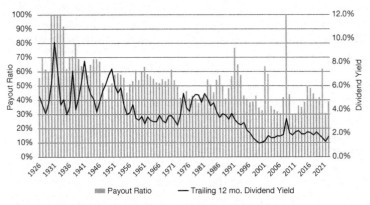

Figure 3.1 U.S. Large-Cap Market Yield and Payout Ratio

Source: Shiller, www.econ.yale.edu/~shiller/data.htm (n.d.)

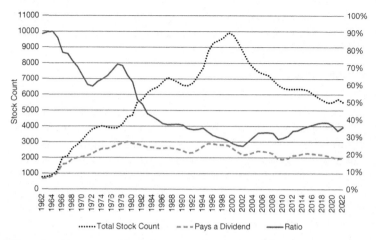

Figure 3.2 Proportion of U.S. Companies that Pay a Dividend

Source: S&P Global Market Intelligence; FactSet, 2023.

Note: Includes all U.S. common stocks in Compustat North America Database with Market Cap. > 0, excludes ADRs and secondary listings.

The same Compustat data can be parsed to see the dividend trends at the individual security level. Whatever the metric, they slope down and to the right. Figure 3.3 uses the top 1,000 companies by market cap—the most investable part of the market. The median yield and the percentage of companies paying dividends decline steadily. In short, until the 1990s dividends mattered. And then they didn't.

As of December 31, 2022, the S&P 500 Index had a trailing cash yield of 1.76%. That's nonsensical from a cash investment or business investment perspective, but such nonsense has been tolerated for years by investors and company executives alike.[1] The stock market's cash yield is now lower than it has been since the modern U.S. stock market started in the early 19th century other than at the very peak of the tech bubble in March 2000. At that time, the S&P 500 Index hit a trailing 12-month yield of 1.1%. Even after the sell-off of 2022, we are not that far away from the all-time low yield. You might think that such a minimal cash return would completely preclude using the U.S. stock

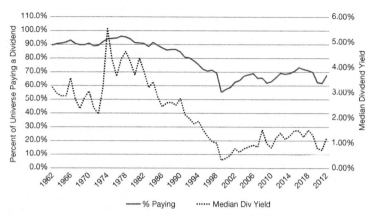

Figure 3.3 Declining Dividends (Among Top 1,000 Companies)

Source: S&P Global Market Intelligence; FactSet, 2023.

Note: Drawn from database of all U.S. common stocks in Compustat North America Database with Market Cap. > 0, excludes ADRs and secondary listings.

market as a traditional business ownership platform. While hard, it is not impossible. That's because the aggregate number is somewhat misleading. The dividend yields, and dividend growth rates vary materially by sector and within sectors. So even during this multi-decade drought, it has been possible to derive a meaningful income stream from the U.S. stock market. It has just been very challenging. That task will become easier with the upcoming paradigm shift.

DECLINING RATES

So what led to this important structural shift in the U.S. stock market and how investors generated returns? The decline in interest rates is the dominant cause. While this book challenges current practices in the stock market and questions numerous shibboleths of academic finance, asserting that the decline in interest rates has had an outsized impact on the U.S. capital markets will ruffle no feathers. Everyone can agree on that. My purpose is simply to call it out and clearly link it to the cash drought of the U.S. stock market.[2] Before doing so, however, it is worth reviewing the importance of one particular interest rate measure—that of the 10-year Treasury Note. Casual stock market investors may find it surprising that so much of the valuation of stocks and the market in general depends on the current rate of interest on U.S. government securities. They are, after all, bonds, not stocks, and have very different attributes. Still, if you've turned on CNBC any morning during the past three decades or glanced at a *Wall Street Journal* summary of market moves in the same period, you will have observed that market participants concentrate a great deal on the yield of the U.S. 10-year Treasury Note, either to forecast the direction of the market or to explain its past movement. If you are in a rush and looking for a single sentiment factor driving the stock market on any given day, ironically, it's not equity-based at all. Check the bond market's pricing of the U.S. 10-year Treasury Note and you will have it.[3]

Why is a particular government bond so important to the stock market? Because the academic formulas dictate it, all serious stock market valuation exercises are based on a discount rate that translates future dividends or earnings back into a price today. That math usually starts with a "risk-free" rate—an intellectually tendentious notion that modern finance has embraced. The idea is that the safest possible investment offers a guaranteed return, something that will not fail. For riskier investments, such as non-U.S. government bonds, high-yield debt, and then equities, investors deserve a premium for taking on the incremental risk of not owning the appropriate government bond. For equities, that is the 10-year Note. (Shorter-maturity investments are benchmarked to shorter-maturity government bonds. Stocks are considered exercises in longer-term discounting and valuation.) The extra risk taken when investing in stocks is called the Equity Risk Premium and is particularly tricky to calculate in real time. (It is readily viewed in retrospect.[4]) This structure of a risk-free rate plus a premium got a boost from the academy in the 1960s in the form of the Capital Asset Pricing Model (CAPM) that made the approach into a simple formula. This shorthand method of calculating an expected return made its way quickly from the academy to the marketplace.

A half-century later, the CAPM is no longer a particularly popular valuation tool, but the CAPM did serve to entrench further the idea that a bond-based, risk-free rate is very important in the valuation of stocks. Because this figure is the only easily and immediately visible component of the equity discount rate on any given day, that bond yield is plastered all over the cable business shows every morning and in most stock market commentaries. Assuming an investor's forecast of stocks' cashflows doesn't change, when the 10-year Note yield moves up, stock prices will decline unless the equity risk premium falls by as much as or more than the yield increase. Conversely, when the 10-year Note yield declines, stock prices will rise unless the equity risk premium gains by as much or more than the 10-year yield has fallen.[5] Of course, the 10-year Note yield doesn't usually move materially unless expectations regarding the economy, especially inflation, have changed. Those altered expectations should eventually affect forecasts of company cashflows, but until those expectations have changed, investors are faced with a toggling back and forth of interest rates, equity risk premia, and share price moves.

While the 10-year Treasury Note is currently the base rate for judging equities, it has not always been so. The U.S. government started issuing 10-year Notes only in 1976, and they became the starting point for risk calculation a few decades later. Before the emergence of the 10-year Note, many analysts used the "long bond," the rate on the U.S. government's 30-year bond. If one goes further back to the early 20th century, before the U.S. Treasury market had not become as liquid as it is now, the base rate (called the "pure interest rate" or "pure rate of interest" prior to the CAPM) was calculated on the yields of the highest quality corporate debt issuers such as American Telephone & Telegraph, General Motors, General Electric, United States Steel, or the Pennsylvania Railroad— those firms assumed always able to meet their obligations within a reasonable investment horizon. The history and significance of the 10-year Treasury Note is worthy of another detailed history. I recommend Edward F. McQuarrie's account of the base bond rates used in the works of Robert Shiller and Jeremy Siegel. For a somewhat dry topic, it makes for a striking mystery read.[6]

This book is not primarily about the valuation of the stock market. So why the extended detour about the 10 year Treasury Note? Because the four-decade decline in the 10-year yield is an important component of the changing structure of the stock market that is the subject here. Its chart back to the early 1960s (using a derived figure prior to 1976) forms a mountain, rising in the post-World War II years and then spiking as inflation dominated the 1970s. Of greater interest is the 40-year decline since the peak in 1981, including more recent periods of negative real (inflation-adjusted) rates. As a result, we've had four decades of a decline in perceived overall risk as the base rate in the formula declined steadily. The drop from the exceptionally high rates in the late 1970s and early 1980s was certainly warranted. Risk at that time was overstated. The question, after a four-decade decline, is whether risk is being properly priced now (and for the past decade or so).[7]

Despite its visibility and simplicity, using the 10-year Note as the starting point to calculate the discount rate for cashflows from stocks is fraught with difficulty. Numerous externalities push and pull the rate around. They include the supply-and-demand dynamics from the U.S. Treasury, an incremental supply-and-demand overlay from foreign buyers, the changing and varied inflation expectations of all market participants, and, for the past decade or so, the active and direct intervention of the Federal Reserve Board. Trying to serve all those masters, the 10-year Note is at best a partial or directional indicator of risk. While most market participants realize that the Fed has had its fingers on the risk scale for many years now, it has been too easy for investors and company managements to point to the 10-year Note to justify dubious and/or heavily indebted ventures.

To get around this flawed construct, I use the term "risk rates" here as a more subjective discounting mechanism to calculate the present value of future cashflows. Modern finance is a mathematical discipline and is unlikely to embrace a non-formulaic approach to risk. But until the "out of order" sign is removed from the official formula, some substitute is needed. The risk rates referenced in this work are more traditional, long-term discount rates expressed in absolute terms—high single digits for large established enterprises and higher, potentially much higher figures for riskier ventures. Much of the financial media earns a living speculating on the future of interest rates. I make no such claim as to the direction of the 10-year Treasury Note. I do claim, however, that after decades of decline, and years of exceptionally low absolute levels, risk rates moved up in the early 2020s and are likely to remain in a more normal range in the years ahead. That is a key component of the paradigm shift outlined in this work. The absolute rates referenced earlier might even be too low if we were to see a material increase in base rates that investors deemed to be structural rather than short-term in nature. While that scenario is unlikely at present, suffice it here and now to say that risk is back.

FALLING RATES AND STOCK MARKET OUTCOMES

Falling interest rates over the past four decades affected the mechanics of the stock market in two ways. The first is straightforward: rates of interest on government securities set the competitive floor for the yield of all bond-like instruments. As government rates rise, other private-sector bonds need to offer a competitive yield to find buyers. As they fall, bonds can pay less and still find customers. The dynamic is similar though not identical for equities. Prior to the 1990s, most stocks had dividends and were judged in terms of their attractiveness, at least partially, by their yield. So, somewhat parallel to bonds, as the yield on government securities moved up or down, the cash return expected from stocks would adjust as well. Even today, in the "post" dividend market, I have been frequently told by company management teams, particularly around spinoffs or mergers of old economy companies where a dividend already exists or is expected, that they are planning on setting the new entity's dividend so that it will have a "competitive" or "attractive" yield. I am always bemused when I hear that as it suggests the executives can control stock prices and therefore determine stock yields. While that is not at all the case, up until the 1990s, investors genuinely did care about the cash yield of stocks. As the yields of the 10-year Treasury Note came down over time, the necessity for stocks to offer high, competitive cash dividend yields diminished.

It is worth recalling that bond coupons and stock dividends are importantly different. The former is an obligation that, if not met, results in dire consequences; the latter is assumed and generally paid but is not a guarantee. The former are also flat for the life of the bond, whereas dividends are expected and regularly do rise over time. This is one of the reasons yields of 1980s stocks were not in the teens. The unusually high bond rates were understood to be temporary, whereas stock income streams are assumed to be permanent, or at least aspire to be so. So while the bond yield puts pressure on stock yields, it is far from a one-to-one relationship. The correlation is undeniable, particularly in the 1980s and 1990s. For the past two decades, however, the market's yield has been relatively steady at very low levels—between 1.5% and 2%—even as the 10-year Note continued to decline to extraordinarily low levels.

While setting the floor for "competitive" cash rates is the first and most straightforward reason for the importance of the risk-free rate, the second is perhaps more important, and that is the aforementioned "risk." As benchmark rates have come down, so too has the discount rate applied to present and prospective cash-flows. That four-decade trend has served to create the almost anything-goes environment that we have observed in the stock market in recent decades. Persistently lower discount rates translate into persistently higher tolerance for risk. This trend goes beyond just the high valuation of cashflows or income streams that is reflected in the S&P 500 Index's low-dividend yield. It also helps explain the existence of entirely dividend-free stocks from large successful companies that can afford to and ought to pay dividends. Consistent with my maxim of business ownership being reflected in a tangible, cash relationship, I view these investments to be "speculations." Without a distributable cash stream, the investor in a successful enterprise is entirely dependent on the ever-changing market price of the investment. That is the dictionary definition of a speculation.

Declining interest rates have expanded the scope for such companies. As of the end of 2022, a stunning 103 companies, representing 19.2% of the S&P 500 Index by market cap, made no distribution. Recall that these are the best of the best—the largest and most successful listed U.S. corporations. They are not start-ups. Even if they are cyclical and at the bottom of a particular business cycle, they are presumed to be durable. Otherwise, they would not be part of the U.S.'s leading stock market index. At any given point in time, some portion of them might reasonably be expected not to pay a dividend due to near-term distress, but not 20% of them. Another 66 companies, with 17.5% of the index's value, trade with a yield of less than a 1% yield. At those levels, the dividend is not a consideration for either investors or management. It has no material present value. That is, roughly 40% of the S&P 500 Index by market cap is dividend-free or so dividend-light that it might as well be dividend-free. That is a stunning state of affairs and a real challenge to an investor seeking to establish a typical, cash-based ownership relationship with investments through the stock market. This dividend desert is particularly noticeable at the top end of the market. The top six companies in the index at the end of 2022 (Apple, Microsoft, Amazon, Berkshire Hathaway, Alphabet, United Health), representing 20% of its total value, had a yield of 1.2% or less.

At the other end of the size spectrum, the challenge is similar. Take, for example, the companies outside the top 500. If you consider companies 501–1,500 (using the S&P 1500 Composite) by market value on December 31, 2022, they had a market cap ranging from $15.1 billion at the high end to $203 million on the low end. These are still large and successful businesses by any reasonable definition measure. Of these 1,000 companies, 417 had no dividend at all. Another 93 were in the less than 1% yield category. So half of these companies offered no means for a traditional cash-based ownership relationship. While there is nothing illegal in not offering investors a dividend, these companies contribute to the impression that the stock market is not supposed to offer cashflow-based investment relationships. Even for investors who don't care particularly about receipt of a dividend, the absence of one deprives all investors of a key traditional measure of valuation. It is harder to say what an asset is worth without a distribution, or one so small it is meaningless. There are so many such companies in the stock market; it should come as no surprise that I—and others—came to consider the U.S. stock market as much "casino" as business ownership platform.

The resulting atmosphere of speculation is not just in terms of the investor who is left only with share price returns. The cashless model also affects management. Low hurdle rates open the door to bad investment decisions by company leaders. While it can be hard to prove at a macro-market level that senior executives are using low cash expectations to overfund projects or make poor investments, it is simple to demonstrate at the behavioral finance level. Free money—nearly free to borrow debt, and similarly low-cost equity when no cash strings are attached—leads exactly to the type of behavior you would expect. If managers actually worked for shareholders and were held accountable by the elected board of directors, this wastage might not be a problem. But in the age of the imperial CEO—and make no mistake, we are living in such an epoch—bad investment decisions are not the preserve of investors only. One form of managerial speculation is in their own shares, the much-vaunted share buybacks.

BUYBACKS

Share buybacks did not cause the dividend retreat, but they rushed in to fill the void left by cash payments to company owners. In doing so, they have changed the math of investing in the stock market. Retiring a company's shares by purchasing them in the open market is not dissimilar from buying out one's partners in a business venture and using the company's cash stockpile to do so. The remaining shareholders own a bigger slice of the same corporate pie (minus the amount of cash used to retire the shares). The trick is that in an open-market environment, the timing and execution of a buyback can look a lot like a company manipulating their share prices. So with the onset of stock market regulation following the Great Depression, buybacks were few and far between as executives sought to avoid drawing the attention of the SEC. The SEC considered loosening the restrictions in 1967, 1970, and 1973, but finally did so in 1982 with the promulgation of SEC rule 10b-18. That rule permitted companies to engage in open-market purchases of their stock as long as they followed a set of stated guidelines designed to make the process somewhat transparent and less likely to move share prices around.

The result of that small regulatory change has been stunning.[8] As shown in Figure 3.4, by the late 1990s, the dollar value of gross buybacks by the top 500 companies exceeded those of dividends and has never looked back, except for a handful of years. While the nominal

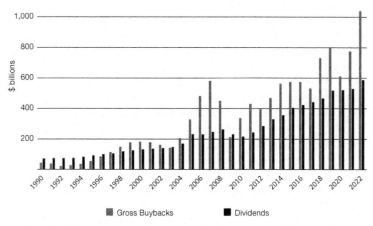

Figure 3.4 S&P 500 Index Aggregate Dividends and Buybacks ($billions)

Source: Société Générale Quantitative Research, 2023.

value of dividends from the index companies has grown nicely, buy-backs are now an equally visible and perhaps even more important component of the current stock market paradigm. With buybacks regularly exceeding dividend payments for S&P 500 Index companies, the market's potential payout ratio and cash yield might be roughly twice what it currently is. That's a huge swing.

Buybacks supplanting dividends tell only part of the story and perhaps not the most important part. From a business owner-ship perspective, buybacks change the ownership calculation, for both the investor and corporate management. I've addressed why that is the case a decade ago in *The Dividend Imperative*. Since it was published, little has changed in Wall Street's and corporate's America's embrace of buybacks over dividends. The argument is worth summarizing here.

First, buybacks are popular because they are believed—by man-agement and some investors—to lead to higher share prices by virtue of having an additional motivated buyer. Second, buybacks demonstrably lift near-term EPS by lowering the denominator in the profit-per-share view of a stock. The benefit depends greatly on whether the funds used are from profits earned or dollars borrowed and the extent to which the denominator needle is moved. However achieved, higher EPS leads to higher compensation for senior managers and higher share prices for investors, assuming valuation "multiples" are maintained. Third, buyback proponents point to the downstream benefits for non-selling shareholders—they get a larger share of the remaining corporate pie, including larger dividends and a greater weight in corporate governance. Fourth, buybacks are purported to be tax efficient in that, compared to a fixed schedule of taxable dividend payments, buybacks can be timed, by both corporations and investors choosing to surrender (sell) their shares. That timing can have a tax benefit for shareholders who are particularly tax averse. Finally, buybacks (along with dividends) are seen as a corporate signaling tool of better times ahead.

The academic clarion call for dividends to disappear occurred before the buyback wave reached its full maturity over the past two decades. Still, one would assume that the academics have embraced buybacks and demonstrated their superiority to dividends. Well, the verdict of the academic literature and real-world experience on all of these supposed virtues is … perhaps.[9] There is no clear evidence that buybacks lead to higher firm values over the long term or represent anything other than a repackaging of a company's productive assets. Buybacks may constitute a short-term demand fillip, for sure. But long-term market trends are generally positive, and correlation is not causation. Buybacks in a market trending up look good; buybacks ahead of a correction look wasteful. The positive EPS effect is well documented; the question is whether the documented reduction in the denominator is anywhere as great as the announcements of these programs suggest. For example, a company with a $1 billion market capitalization announces, with great fanfare, a $100 million buyback that will—in theory—reduce the shares outstanding by 10%. The remaining shareholders will see their relative stakes in the company rise by 11%. But there are a lot of steps between announcement and realization. Companies often announce large repurchase programs, but they are under no obligation to complete them. If the market price of the shares rises during a repurchase program—in theory, a good thing—the number of shares that can be repurchased with the same dollars declines. And finally, as shares are being retired through the repurchase program, they are often being issued to employees, reducing the sharecount-reduction benefit of the program. In that instance, buybacks are essentially part of corporate compensation programs. Indeed, many corporate buyback efforts are designed just to offset those grants to employees. Those buybacks benefit investors by virtue of a well-designed compensation program that helps retain key employees, but they are not intended specifically to reward shareholders with cash.

And then there is a dark side to repurchases, which many companies may learn the hard way in the years to come. Share repurchases financed from debt have been popular as interest rates have come down over the decades. Indeed, the math of corporations borrowing cheaply to buy back their own shares can appear irresistible. With rates no longer declining, it's not clear that that benefit will remain. Engineering growth through buybacks financed from cheap debt is not organic growth. Buyer beware. I'm not saying anything that is new. The mixed results of buybacks are well known, but their allure to corporate executives, brokerages, and hedge funds is undeniable. After three decades, buybacks are embedded in the fabric of the market, for better or for worse.

Still, let's consider the broader implications of buybacks from a business ownership perspective. They are part and parcel of the shift in definition of market success from distributions-based—the dividends paid—to a nearly exclusive focus on the share price. It also redefines a company's relationship to the capital markets. Rather than having the capital markets reflect the value of the company—the collective wisdom of investors—share prepurchase programs make companies into market participants, that is, above and beyond their supposed core competence of widget making. There may be nothing wrong with that, but investors should be aware of how the investment process—the supposed valuation mechanism of the stock market—has been altered in the process.

Other critics have pointed out that buybacks further the "financialization" of the capital markets by changing the investment optics of a company without actually changing its productive capacity. In a way, these modern critics are repeating the excellent point made by M&M 60 years ago that a business's earnings potential, not how the assets are packaged, should drive its market valuation. Buybacks challenge that bit of common sense. For brokerages, hedge funds, and speculators, these new optics are wonderful developments; for investors seeking to benefit from the ownership dividend, buybacks simply muddy the waters. In contrast, dividends are an expected and a natural outcome of a successful commercial enterprise—where the focus is on the company and its operations—as opposed to financial engineering, where the focus is whatever shuffling of the deck is needed to always deal out a full house or better.

My point here is not to make an argument against buybacks. That's a topic for another book. Instead, the business owner operating through the stock market once again needs to appreciate the difference between a company dollar distributed as a dividend, and one spent in the stock market. It is the same difference between a dividend and harvested capital gain that I referenced earlier. Academic finance treats the two as the same. In a similar fashion, corporate managements and Wall Street have convinced investors that dividends and buybacks are very similar and fit under the umbrella of "returning cash to shareholders." Both assumptions are wrong. A dividend is a business outcome; the other—whether a harvested capital gain or a buyback—is a market outcome. They are really quite remote from one another. Do not be persuaded otherwise by someone whose compensation depends on the success of a specious argument.

THE RISE OF NASDAQ AND SILICON VALLEY

In any review of the market in the 1920s and 1930s, one can find reference to growth stocks. That is not hard. And they were not necessarily treated as speculations, though many were. But at that time, there were no style benchmarks and no universe of growth products that could be measured and analyzed. So the analysis of growth investing in the 1920s and 1930s is anecdotal at best. That begins to change in the postwar period, especially in the 1950s and through the 1960s, when we see the emergence of growth as an explicit investment style, not just the characterization of individual listings. Having founded his own investment management business in 1937, T. Rowe Price was enthusiastically picking "growth stocks" for his clients by the 1950s. The firm launched what they consider the nation's first growth fund—the Trowe Price Growth Stock Fund—at the beginning of that decade. The securities held there almost certainly had dividends. Growth was not in opposition to dividends; it was just growth. At the time, the market—defined as the precursor to the S&P 500 Index—yielded around 7%, yes, 7%. Whatever the growth fund's yield was, I am confident that it was not zero.

During the same decade, investment advisor Philip Fisher hit it big with his *Common Stocks and Uncommon Profits*, published in 1958. His message was simple and well tuned for the times: buy growing companies. There was lots of growth to be had in the 1950s and 1960s. Postwar America was prosperous and on an economic roll, so the emergence of growth stocks and growth investing wasn't that surprising. The specific "performance investing" culture that emerged by the 1960s (and was so well captured by the journalists John Brooks and George Goodman) was all about prices going up sharply and quickly. What may come as more of a surprise is that, generally speaking, these growth companies had dividends. The payout ratios and yields might have been less, but they were still there. Clearly, dividends had taken a back seat, but they were still a part of the equation.

As to the exact nature of the equation, the academics were playing catchup in the 1950s and 1960s. They seemed to struggle with one overarching question—how to value growth stocks. It was hard then; it's hard now. The numerous new investing and finance journals were filled with their efforts. As they grapple with valuing growth, the cashflows received by the shareholders in the form of dividends are still a major point of the exercise. They do not posit stocks without dividends. Yes, the payout ratio was lower than non-growth stocks to allow reinvestment, but it was far from zero. And the dividend was still a central part of the actual valuation equation.

The Nasdaq exchange started in the early 1970s as a computerized means of showing bid and offer prices among dealers for shares not listed on the major exchanges. The earliest Nasdaq system wasn't actually a trading mechanism, but an information-sharing tool that allowed dealers from all over the country to engage in basic price discovery. Transactions still occurred over the phone, person to person. That would soon change as Nasdaq evolved into the trading system that we use today. Today, Nasdaq has around 3,000 listings, more than the older NYSE. The market value of the listed shares on Nasdaq is around $17.5 trillion, in a league with the NYSE's $25 trillion.[10] Most institutional and retail investors wouldn't know the difference between the two exchanges, though their operations are not identical. But the experience in buying, selling, or owning shares on either exchange is virtually indistinguishable. For investors, whether shares are listed on the Nasdaq or the NYSE is a back-office issue; for companies choosing to list their shares on one or the other exchange—they do have distinct listing requirements—it is also a matter of preference, not a fundamental difference.

While the listing exchange matters little, Nasdaq has passed into our investment culture and reality as an entire investment type: innovative technology-oriented enterprises, many located in the Bay Area of Northern California. These Silicon Valley companies have changed the world, full stop. We all know the names: Amazon, Apple, Google, Meta (the parent of Facebook), Microsoft, Cisco, Amgen, etc. For the past 50 years, these companies had their initial public offerings and raised additional capital, if needed, overwhelmingly on the Nasdaq exchange. In doing so, they have changed not only modern life but also the stock market itself. Whereas the payment of dividends was the *sine qua non* of success for companies on the NYSE, it is the opposite for those listed on Nasdaq. Dividends are an infrequent occurrence. Of the top 500 companies on the exchange as of December 31, 2022, only 42% paid a dividend at all. The smallest of these 500 companies has a market capitalization of $2.9 billion—with a "b"—so they are by no means insignificant, troubled enterprises.[11] With more than half the dataset not having a dividend, the median yield is zero, of course. And when weighted by market cap, the yield of the top 500 Nasdaq companies was just 1.06%. Why bother.

There are any number of reasonable explanations as to why Nasdaq is essentially a dividend-free zone. Its initial heritage—the place for rapidly growing technology companies with full investment agendas—is certainly the leading one. That would explain why the younger, less-established companies appearing on the Nasdaq would naturally eschew dividends in favor of investing every spare dollar they have. Of the largest 500 companies on the exchange, 136 reported losing money in 2022. Whether in that year, or any year in the past, money-losing enterprises would reasonably not make distributions. A total of 173 had free cashflow of less than $100 million. It might or might not be reasonable to expect a dividend from them. These companies, however, are the exception to the Nasdaq rule. The larger Nasdaq listings—the top 300 or so—are, by definition, tremendously successful, and yet they continue to not reward company owners in cash. Of course, to some extent they do not need to, as investors are willing to take their chips in the form of abundant capital gains—notwithstanding one burst bubble two decades ago and the sell-off of 2022.

There are other factors as well. I wonder if distance from New York and "old finance" isn't one of them. Timing most certainly is. Nasdaq came of age in the 1980s and 1990s, by which time M&M's "dividend irrelevance" of 1961 had morphed into a free pass to ignore dividends no matter how large and successful an enterprise was. Nasdaq's later start also allowed its constituent members to be incorporated into Modern Portfolio Theory, which itself focused so much on share price co-variances and so little on dividend payments.[12]

Big Tech is now under siege from the left and the right for having become too powerful, too successful, and too dominant. It's a good problem to have. But it is not the issue here. (I actually like Facebook and am willing to state that in print. It suits my Baby-Boomer social media needs almost perfectly.) The issue is how the emergence of a vast coterie of large, successful, cashflow-generating companies has changed the investing equation in the United States. Let's return to the top 500 Nasdaq issues, the best of the best. At the aggregate level, the companies can surely cut much larger checks to their shareholders. For the year ending December 31, 2022, net income was $580 billion, while dollar dividends amounted to a measly $172 billion. Taking into consideration depreciation and capital expenditures—the former at $315 billion and the latter at $405 billion—free cashflow before dividends becomes $589 billion, more than $400 billion greater than the dividend obligation. Share buybacks in 2022 amounted to $494 billion, nearly three times the amount spent on dividends. These aggregate numbers are dominated by the handful of companies at the top of the leaderboard. This is not just a matter of the FAANGs and the usual Big Tech suspects. They have obvious and massive cashflows and the ability to establish a material cash relationship with their owners. But consider the rest of the Nasdaq success stories. At the individual company level, of the 500 largest companies on the exchange, 268–54% by count and 81% by market value have Net Income and Free Cashflow (Net Income + Depreciation—Capital Expenditure) of greater than $100 million. Of those companies—all of which can and should be paying cash to company owners—only 156 (58%) do. And the dividend pay-out ratio (of net income) for those distributions is just 32%.[13] They could do a lot more. And in the years ahead, I believe, they will have to do a lot more to compete for investors on a cash basis.

IMPLICATIONS

If you build a casino, they will come. The collective impact of falling rates, rising share buybacks, and the great success of Silicon Valley has transformed the nature of investment and business ownership through the stock market. The process occurred gradually. Decades ago, investors were put into a market of then room-temperature water. Had they been presented with the zero-dividend option, it would have been a shock to them and they would have jumped from the pot as quickly as a frog. But over the years, the temperature has risen slowly but steadily, and investors have stayed, until they are now used to stocks—even large, highly successful, highly profitable enterprises—with no or *de minimis* dividends. That in turn has changed the stock market equation for most investors. All but a small coterie of investors now look almost entirely to share price gains as a measure of their businesses' success, not the cash distributions they receive from their ownership stake. While there is nothing per se wrong with that measurement tool, investors should appreciate how different it is from the measure of success in private business, or earlier iterations of the stock market.

Time horizons have been reduced. There have always been speculators who come to play the casino to make a "quick buck." All markets are such. But dividend-focused investing is by definition longer-term in nature as investors are looking out to a stream of payments over time. Assets stripped of such payments make investors entirely dependent on share price movements alone, and those can occur in days and weeks, rather than years. The topic of short termism—its impact on companies and investors—is well known. It is simply a matter here of pointing out that the move from a cash market to a nearly cashless one has greatly accentuated the problem.

Dividend payments also dampen total return volatility of individual investments because a portion of a stock's annual total return appears steadily and more or less predictably. The absence of those regular payments leaves investors entirely dependent on the whims of the market and other investors. The difference between the two experiences is crystal clear in the stock market over the past three decades, as indicated in Figure 3.5. High-dividend-paying securities have a much lower standard deviation—a smoother ride—than the dividend-free, stock-price-only roller coaster rides.[14] The gap has narrowed in the recent decade as investors got used to dividend-free stocks as investments rather than speculations.

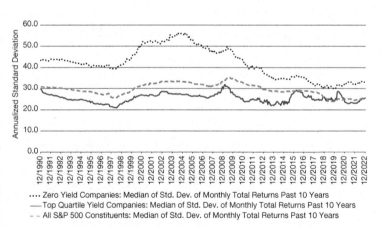

•••• Zero Yield Companies: Median of Std. Dev. of Monthly Total Returns Past 10 Years
——— Top Quartile Yield Companies: Median of Std. Dev. of Monthly Total Returns Past 10 Years
– – All S&P 500 Constituents: Median of Std. Dev. of Monthly Total Returns Past 10 Years

Figure 3.5 Standard Deviation Medians: High-Dividend Stocks versus Non-Dividend Stocks

Source: S&P Global Market Intelligence; FactSet, 2023.

For many investors, that roller coaster ride has worked just fine, especially when the price chart is up and to the right, as it has been for most of the past 30 years. There are times, however, such as 2022, when the chart is down and to the right, sharply for many of the darlings of the prior five years. This is not to suggest that dividend-paying stocks can't sell off dramatically, but the non-paying companies do seem more prone to hitting big air pockets.

Consider, for example, the following case of a popular new-economy media streaming company versus an old-economy utility. Their five-year price charts through the end of 2022 and return figures are shown in Figure 3.6. Total return is about the same, but they got there in very different ways.

Ticker	Name	Price Return	Total Return	Annualized Total Return	Standard Deviation of Monthly Total Returns
NFLX	Netflix Inc.	53.6%	53.6%	9.0%	12.9%
DUK	Duke Energy	22.5%	50.8%	8.6%	5.3%

Figure 3.6 Netflix versus Duke Comparative Total Returns, 2018-2022

Source: FactSet financial data and analytics, 2023.

I suppose it depends on what you want. Traders and hedge funds will prefer the wild ride of the media streaming company. Business owners investing through the stock market should, all other factors held equal, prefer the coupon-clipping, coupon-growing experience of the utility.

There is also a political angle. As we have seen in the past few years, stocks can and are owned for reasons utterly unrelated to dividends or even "buy low, sell high" stock market reasons. Stripped of a critical valuation mechanism, stocks can be anything the investor wants them to be, up to and including political statements. The recent GameStop phenomenon, covered by Spencer Jakab in his insightful *The Revolution That Wasn't*, makes it quite clear that the motivations of the players involved had more to do with political economy than with business ownership or stock valuation. Sure, it is possible to own a high-dividend-paying business to make a political statement, but the overall market environment has led to more stocks being viewed as playthings rather than serious exercises in business ownership.

Finally, the prior cash-based market also used to provide a vetting mechanism that has now been removed. I leave it to the ever-so-honest brokers and investment bankers of Wall Street to determine whether too many companies without profits or the prospect of profits (or even revenues) have made it to the public markets. With no cash obligation to investors, it is no doubt easier to raise capital than it probably ought to be. Critics will object that the stock market is precisely the right platform for investors to take risk and allocate capital to emerging companies. I have no disagreement there, though the venture capital world has done most of the entrepreneurial heavy lifting for the past few decades. The issue for investors in the public markets is distinguishing between larger cashflow-generative companies and their lesser, younger peers. When one can and does pay a dividend, it helps differentiate the two. When neither does, it can be that much harder.

For all its virtues, the Nasdaq revolution over the past four decades has helped drain the stock market of its cash payments. Without questioning the Silicon Valley innovation engine, I do assert that its success is certainly not due to holding back profit distributions to company owners once the enterprises had grown to size and scale.

There is little evidence to suggest otherwise. So much of Nasdaq is outside the bounds of M&M, where a choice between investment and distributions has to be made. So not paying a dividend is a choice, not a necessity. Will that election remain the same for the biggest Nasdaq companies in the decades ahead? My belief is no, and that even Silicon Valley companies will have to treat company owners as they are treated in every other business setting. Investors in the tech sector will do well to seek out those companies that can and will "normalize" their relations with investors in the years to come.

***

So that's where we are today. Fortuna's Wheel of investing has turned 180 degrees, and the dividend-collector Boethius is not particularly happy. He takes little Consolation from this state of affairs. It is worth observing, however, that nothing in the current arrangement is illegal in an SEC sense. And much of the current investment framework has been blessed by the share price-focused academy. It is certainly supported enthusiastically by the financial services industry. But for dividend-focused investors, there is utility in knowing how we got here, and that we can now be seen as the outsider, the underdog, perhaps even the innovator in investments. We are zigging when everyone else is zagging. We use the stock market to generate income when everyone else is focused on the share prices. Even under the current adverse circumstances, it is possible to generate a meaningful income stream from a diversified portfolio of stocks. In the next chapter, I describe how.

NOTES

[1] The yields of the German and Japanese markets have also been low decades for somewhat similar (and somewhat different) reasons.

[2] I touched upon the implications of falling rates, while they were still falling, in an earlier treatment. Since then, more than a decade ago, interest and risk rates continued to decline (until the early 2020s), making the issue even more acute than when I originally addressed it. Daniel Peris, *Strategic Dividend Investor* (New York: McGraw-Hill, 2011), 66–69.

[3] Changes in shorter-term interest rates usually have an immediate impact on the share prices of banks because rate movements correlate directly to a bank's Net Interest Margin, a key source of its operating profit.

[4] Professor Aswath Damodaran maintains a regularly updated database of equity risk premia: www.stern.nyu.edu/~adamodar/pc/datasets/histimpl.xls.

[5] On any given day, the phenomenon can be reversed. A sharp "risk off" day involves a rush from equities into the relative security of government bonds, pushing yields down; a "risk on" day sees investors funding the purchase of stocks with the sale of government bonds, pushing their yields up. But over the long term, it has been steadily declining rates of interest and rising appetites for risk.

[6] Edward F. McQuarrie, "When Do Corporate Bond Investors Earn a Premium for Bearing Risk? A Test Spanning the Great Depression of the 1930s," (December 2020). Available at SSRN: https://ssrn.com/abstract=3740190.

[7] Market Yield on the U.S. Treasury Securities at 10-Year Constant Maturity, Quoted on an Investment Basis (DGS10) | FRED | St. Louis Fed (stlouisfed.org), set to maximum period. See also Edward Chancellor, *The Price of Time: The Real Story of Interest* (New York: Atlantic Monthly Press, 2022) on the broader implications of excessively low rates of interest.

[8] For an earlier analysis of the buyback phenomenon, see Daniel Peris, *The Dividend Imperative* (New York: McGraw-Hill, 2013), 45–81.

[9] The ambiguity is captured rather brilliantly by Clifford Asness, Todd Hazelkorn, and Scott Richardson in their "Buyback Derangement Syndrome," *Journal of Portfolio Management*, Vol. 44, no. 5 (Spring 2018), 50–57. The JSTOR database holds scores of articles from the past decade on the virtues and shortcomings of share buybacks. That's the point.

[10] As of 31 December, 2022.

[11] There are "pre-revenue" and pre-profit companies in the top 500 Nasdaq. They would not be expected to pay a dividend.

[12] As argued in the author's *Getting Back to Business* (2018).

[13] All data from the Compustat database of S&P Global Market Intelligence and FactSet, 2023.

[14] S&P Global Market Intelligence using the Compustat database, and Factset, 2023. For each constituent of the S&P 500 Index, the annualized standard deviation of monthly total returns for the prior 120 months is calculated at each date. The companies are then sorted into three groups: (1) all constituents of the S&P 500, (2) constituents of the S&P 500 that do not pay a dividend, and (3) constituents of the S&P 500 that are in the top quartile in terms of dividend yield. Finally, at each date the average and median of the annualized standard deviations are calculated for each group.

4

BEING A DIVIDEND INVESTOR IN A STOCK MARKET

THE CURRENT INVESTMENT FRAMEWORK

In our low-yielding market, it is easy to dismiss high-dividend-focused portfolios as a simple style choice, without a distinct investment framework. For the casual observer, dividend-focused investing may appear to be just one of many "factor" choices that have dominated investment analysis since the 1960s. You know them as growth, value, earnings momentum, beta, size, and dozens upon dozens of other characteristics that can be identified. To the extent dividend-focused investing is considered at all, it is usually viewed as a subset of the broader discipline of value investing, at which point all roads lead to the doorstep of Messrs. Buffett and Munger in Omaha, Nebraska. And so the discussion starts and ends. From my perspective, the all-important but missing "factor" isn't one of these quantitative characteristics at all, but the philosophy of business ownership underpinning dividend-focused portfolios. That this philosophy is disregarded as a consideration in modern investment analysis speaks volumes about how far removed the U.S. stock market has become from traditional business investment practices. We'll take up that

DOI: 10.4324/9781003292272-5

philosophical challenge in the following section. In this chapter, I describe how dividend investing gets done, despite the inauspicious environment.

A LIMITED OPPORTUNITY SET AS THE DEFAULT INVESTMENT FRAMEWORK

The U.S. market's evolution over the past three decades into a nearly cashless investment platform, leaving dividends as "just" a boutique option (or a minor subset of value), has relegated dividend investing into a default investment framework. When only a small portion of the market still has material dividends, that reduced opportunity set defines the style. Circa 2023, this approach entails robust exposure to utilities, phone companies, pipelines, integrated energy, regional commercial banks, large pharma, selected real estate investment trusts (REITs), and consumer staples. It means less exposure to information technology, consumer discretionary, highly cyclical industrials, and materials.

The framework is then built around what drives these sectors. And for most of the time and most of the companies, that is basic economic activity. There is no good measure of such activity, though GDP is the accepted proxy and has been for decades. Dividend-focused companies consume GDP and generate dividends from it. It is an investment exercise built around small-sum purchases made by millions of consumers on a daily, weekly, and monthly basis: grocery shopping, filling the tank, paying the phone and utilities bills, getting prescriptions filled, engagements with the bank, etc.

Getting dividends from the enterprises at the center of these transactions necessarily involves company-specific analysis. Do the individual companies have the right products, scale, market share opportunity, a manageable capital intensity, sustainable margins, reasonable indebtedness, the commitment to shareholders to pay dividends, a payout ratio that makes for a meaningful income stream for company owners? Perhaps most importantly, after a 40-year period of declining rates, offshoring, and the move to services from manufacturing, are these companies investing enough in their future and still be able to keep faith with investors by distributing a share of the profits to investors? This can't be answered definitively in each case, but it can be answered for enough companies to create a diversified portfolio of material dividend-paying companies. It is an exercise in the "fundamental analysis" talked about on Wall Street, but rather than being applied to next quarter's often subjective "earnings," it is focused on a company's ability and inclination to pay objective dividends to shareholders for years to come.

This is not to suggest that there is no macroeconomic or macro-market investment framework for the dividend investor. Depending on the portfolio and the companies held, forces other than basic consumer demand may have an impact on near- or intermediate-term dividend growth. They include currency (for the multinationals or foreign holdings), the price of oil and gas to heat the house and fill the tank, and the interest rates that set the cost of consumer borrowing. But these macro-factors matter less than just the base-level economic activity. That means that the portfolio manager or end investor doesn't have to sweat as much when the ADP employment number, or the Empire State Manufacturing survey, or the Fed minutes, or the Purchasing Managers Index (PMI), or any of the other numerous macro-numbers come out. Those news tidbits and data points matter a great deal more to cyclical companies in cyclical portfolios. There is nothing wrong with cyclicality and volatility, but in its current constitution, the high-yielding corner of the U.S. stock market is less exposed to those "factors." It is not unexposed; it is just less exposed.

DIVIDEND YIELD

But what about the actual math of the portfolio? Businesses have various purposes, but at the end of the day, they need to meet their costs and then some if they are to survive and prosper. The "then some" can be reinvested to attempt to grow the business further, can be distributed to company owners, or split to achieve both goals. If you don't agree with that basic notion, you're probably not reading this far. There are B Corps[1] (and of course non-profit enterprises); they have different goals. But they are a distinct minority in the business landscape. Stakeholder capitalism is making inroads in Europe. It is an alternative framework, but one not yet widely accepted in the United States.

So how does a portfolio of dividend-focused stocks "make money"? By paying and growing the dividends. Those actions generate the total return that investors seek from any investment. It operates on several levels. The most obvious is the yield, the cash payments received from the companies divided by the price for said payments at any moment in time. That's fairly straightforward. The U.S. market yields around 1.5% and has yielded less than 2% for more than two decades. Given the opportunity set, a reasonably concentrated portfolio of mostly S&P 500 Index companies plus a few foreign names with large operations in the United States can produce a portfolio yielding around 4%. It can be higher; it can be lower. It depends on the companies the investor wants and the resulting incremental risks or exposures. This sort of material yield necessarily comes with a high payout ratio of profits and cashflow. Investors with other preferences will look askance at high payout companies as handcuffing management. They are right. A high payout does limit management options. And from the perspective of this minority shareholder, that's a very good thing. Company managers with no cash obligation to shareholders behave exactly as you would expect them. (As discussed later in this work, Michael Jensen in 1976 and again in 1986 directly addresses this issue.) There is an agency cost to being a minority shareholder. A high-dividend payout is the shareholder's trump card.

While the yield changes with the daily repricing of stocks (versus only annual adjustments to dividends, in most cases), it is broadly steady over time for securities that are in the non-cyclical part of the economy and market. That is, high-yielding companies tend to stay high yielders, at least on a relative basis. And low or non-yielding ones stay there as well. Part of that steadiness is due to investor preferences, and partly due to management's choice to be known as a strong (or non-)dividend payer.

DIVIDEND GROWTH

Yield is just the first step. The more interesting and challenging part is dividend growth. It comes in several forms. The first is organic, when individual companies increase their distributions as their businesses grow over time. That dividend growth propels share prices as investors react to the increase by pushing prices back to what they consider an appropriate yield. Younger stock market participants will be surprised to hear that share prices follow the dividend trajectory. But from a business ownership perspective, it is hardly a radical concept. The value of an enterprise increases in line with the trajectory of its distributable cashflows. Even from a stock market perspective, for those companies that have been long-term dividend payers, the correlation is notably high: share prices follow the dividend (or expectations of its future path), plus or minus minor changes in valuation multiples.

The correlation between dividend growth and share price was initially addressed in *The Dividend Imperative*, from 2013.[2] In Figures 4.1–4.4, I have provided a different perspective (and another decade of data). For the "class of 1972" through the end of 2022, companies with meaty dividends at the time and still paying dividends a half-century later have a very high correlation between share price gains and dividend growth. (This is designed and acknowledged as an exercise in survivorship bias. That's the point.) It is the same with the class of 1982 and even 1992. The correlations weaken in the 21st century as the anything-goes mentality takes over.[3] Note as well that the y-intercept is notably positive in each case. As interest and risk rates fell for much of the period under review, yields were coming down across the board, even for high-dividend stocks. That is, we have all become accustomed to paying more (cash) for less (cash). I expect that trend to reverse in the years ahead. The scatter plots from 2022 to 2032 or 2042 will show the vast majority of stocks with dividend growth in excess of share price gains. (They will be below the perfect diagonal, in the lower, shaded area.) For the current zero or *de minimis* payers, that is not a particularly brave forecast, but I also expect to see it for the current payers.

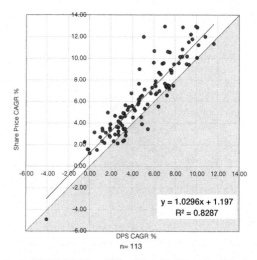

Figure 4.1 Annual DPS CAGR vs Share Price CAGR 12/31/1972–12/31/2022:
For top 50% of all Active Dividend Paying Stocks on Compustat
Database 1972–2022 in terms of 1972 Dividend Yield

Source: S&P Global Market Intelligence; FactSet, 2023.

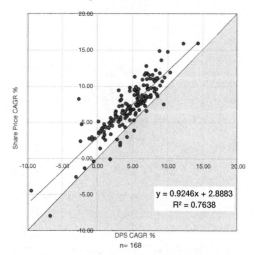

Figure 4.2 Annual DPS CAGR vs Share Price CAGR 12/31/1982–12/31/2022:
For top 50% of all Active Dividend Paying Stocks on Compustat
Database 1982–2022 in terms of 1982 Dividend Yield

Source: S&P Global Market Intelligence; FactSet, 2023.

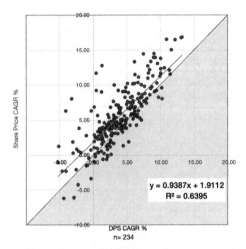

Figure 4.3 Annual DPS CAGR vs Share Price CAGR 12/31/1992–12/31/2022:
For top 50% of all Active Dividend Paying Stocks on Compustat
Database 1992–2022 in terms of 1992 Dividend Yield

Source: S&P Global Market Intelligence; FactSet, 2023.

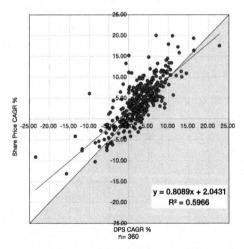

Figure 4.4 Annual DPS CAGR vs Share Price CAGR 12/31/2002–12/31/2022:
For top 50% of all Active Dividend Paying Stocks on Compustat
Database 2002–2022 in terms of 2002 Dividend Yield

Source: S&P Global Market Intelligence; FactSet, 2023.

Academic finance nerds will remind me that correlation is not causation. In this case, however, it probably is. First, 50 years of data means few other factors even have the option of playing a role. That's the intentional survivorship bias. Second, common sense links the value and trajectory of an enterprise's distributable cashflows to its value in the market. More means higher; less means lower. One could counter that it is earnings, not dividends, that drive share prices. And in 1972 that might have been the case. At that time, dividends and earnings were more or less synonymous. Read your original Ben Graham. But in the decades since, earnings have moved to the best-selling fiction shelf, while dividends have remained in the often-overlooked nonfiction section. That weakening correlation between dividend growth and share price gains in recent decades (and the narrowing opportunity set) has contributed to the challenge of being a dividend investor in a stock market. Obviously, the legion of major stocks without dividends is driven by other forces. Suffice it here to acknowledge that share price gains over time driven by sustainable dividend growth are remote from the buy low, sell high, work-the-casino investment framework for non- or low-dividend stocks.

Rising dividends create interesting consequences, whether from individual companies or a portfolio of them. One of them is the distinction between nominal and real (inflation-adjusted) growth. Investors have gotten out of the habit of distinguishing between the two. In the low-inflationary environment we have had until recently, the distinction was unimportant. Nominal and real growth were essentially the same. That is no longer the case. Investors will need to keep two sets of return figures in their heads. Dividend growth is important in this regard as it can be a mechanism to offset modest inflation. I don't want to suggest that dividend growth from equities is the perfect inflation nullifier. As we've seen over the past few years, inflation is first and foremost a headwind to the operations of large enterprises. Companies have to combat inflation by managing their costs and eventually by raising prices. Over time, however, nominal dividend growth rates will track, plus or minus, inflation. Dividend growth above inflation, as we've seen in recent decades, is wonderful; it is real creation of wealth. But over much longer time horizons, real stock market returns have not been too far from the dividend yield itself, with inflation offsetting much of the dividend growth. That is why it is so important to have a material up-front cashflow from one's mature investments.

Getting dividend growth from an already high-yielding portfolio is hard. And that's the main challenge for the committed dividend investor in today's dividend-light stock market. The market is filled with so-called dividend growth funds, ETFs, and SMAs, but they are somewhat misnamed. Many of them have low—often very low—starting yields and higher (high-single-digit or better) dividend growth rates. There is nothing wrong with that approach, but it is fair to call out that the low starting yield completely knee-caps the Net Present Value (NPV) of the dividend stream. And in a rising rate environment, the "little now, more later" approach is also duration-challenged. Rising or high interest rates take a much bigger bite out of the future cashflows than present ones. (Duration in dividend-focused portfolios is addressed in greater detail in Chapter 8.)

Yield on cost is an important means of appreciating the challenge and opportunity of dividend growth. Let's say an investor puts $1 million in a portfolio yielding 4% (net of fees) and where the portfolio's dividend grows 6% steadily over five years. When the dividend is taken by the investor, the yield on cost after five years of dividend growth is an impressive 5.35% compared to the original 4%. The real beauty of compounding occurs when the investor can initially afford to reinvest the dividends. In that case, the yield on cost after five years of compounding is 6.51%. (The reinvested dividends purchase shares that have appreciated at the rate of the dividend growth so that the yield for the newly purchased shares remains steady at 4%.) Hold a solid dividend payer and grower for a decade or more and the yield on cost can easily be well into double digits. Investors who have the luxury of holding securities for decades in preparation for their retirement and then drawing the income off the portfolio can have dividends greater than the purchase price of the security, a yield on cost above 100%. Imagine owning a piece of property that, during the course of your ownership, ends up generating distributable profits greater than the price paid. It is important to keep in mind real and nominal returns here—real returns analysis would dampen the exuberance. Still, yield-on-cost exercises for a rising dividend portfolio are impressive.

Organic dividend growth is the foundation of a portfolio's growth over time, but "accretive" trading is another source of increasing the distributions of a portfolio over time, and therefore augmenting the NPV of the investment. The commentary heretofore has been static. It assumes generally stable yields from individual securities and no trading. That is unrealistic. The market is open 250 days a year. While in an ideal world, no trading would be necessary for the business owner working through the stock market, in the world we live in—with lots of mispricing and plenty of shifting investor preferences for different styles—stocks go in and out of favor with little if any change to the company's long-term dividend trajectory. That creates the opportunity to increase cashflow to company owners. Let me explain. You buy Acme Widget Company for $100 per share. It has a $4 annual dividend. The dividend grows around 5% per year. Over time, one would expect the share price to grow by roughly the same amount. Expected total return is around 9% per year. But in any given week, quarter, or year, the share price can be all over the place. For instance, if widget makers are suddenly in great demand and investors push up the price of Acme by 50% in six months, the company is now yielding 2.67% for new investors or reinvested dividends. It would take many years of 5% dividend increases for the distribution to "catch up" with that share price and return the yield to 4%. But if another buyer can be found at $150 per share, the income-savvy maximizer will consider selling. The proceeds can then be put into a different security yielding 4%, for a new income stream of $6 per year, a big increase over the earlier $4 annual payment. That's an extreme example of an accretive trade, and one that rarely occurs outside of sectors such as energy or banks, but lesser moves of 25% in any given year can occur in any sector. And it's a source of distribution growth that is not available to passive, index-based products. Accretive trading sounds simple, but it is not. One can get trades wrong, there are trading costs, etc. And the math works in reverse just as easily. Decretive trades can turn a robust income stream into a smaller one. So the income maximizing investor seeks a balance of mostly long-term business ownership, complemented by an appropriate amount—less is always better—of accretive trading.

Accretive trading activity can sound somewhat random—not part of a disciplined investment framework—but it is not. That is because of the currently constrained dividend opportunity set. Core holdings such as phone companies and utilities and certain other steady-Eddie businesses are less subject to accretive trading because their yield moves only in a narrow range as their dividends rise over time. But certain financials and industrials and consumer staples, whose yields "come and go" into and out of the dividend investor's sweet spot, can constitute great material for accretive trades.

MANAGING DIVIDEND CUTS

If dividend growth is so important to this particular investment framework, what about companies that cut their dividends? At first glance, the answer is easy: Get rid of them! But as in so many other spheres of business management, the answer is not so simple. Managing a high-yielding portfolio in a low-yielding market necessarily means taking dividend risk. Every once in a while, a mistake will be made by either the investor or a company, leading to a holding cutting its distribution. The goal is to minimize those instances, but they will still occur. Though having a company cut its distribution looks bad, the impact on a portfolio of 30–50 such companies is usually minimal. One can always reduce the risk of an individual company cut by getting rid of the highest yielding security in the portfolio, or even the highest three or four of them. But then other companies top the list and pose a similar if slightly smaller risk. The only way to fully avoid the risk of having cuts in the portfolio is to hold such a low-yielding portfolio that the dividend represents only a small portion of profits. But at that point, the yield of the holdings and the portfolio as a whole would be so miserly as to be meaningless. Nothing ventured; nothing gained. So for a narrative boost—"we are 'dividend aristocrats'; we have never reduced the dividend in 25 years!"—it is quite possible you have left cash on the table.

For the past several decades, the low-yield, high-dividend growth approach has had the wind at its back. It has generated very attractive total returns even if the distributed cashflows have been modest. But as a business owner operating through the stock market, my goal is to maximize the cashflows, not the narrative. So we accept dividend risk as part of the dividend investment framework. Indeed, the logic of maximizing portfolio income can mean adding to a position of a company that has just reduced its distribution. What's done is done; it is a sunk cost. If the outlook for the company is improved as a result of the action, then adding to it might make sense. Seeing your holdings as businesses rather than just stocks is another way of putting the occasional dividend cut in context. Do you sell a rental property where the income stream from it has declined one year? Possibly, if you feel the rental stream will not recover. But if you see a better future after the rough patch, you might keep it, or even invest more in the property. Now the stock market usually makes a hash of share prices where companies are facing genuine dividend risk, both prior to and immediately after a cut. So the decision to exit, maintain, or increase a position is not an easy one. The important factor is taking a long-term view and considering the prospective or historical dividend cut within the context of the overall portfolio's future income stream.

RATIOS AND MEASURES: IRR

That's the summary version of a dividend-focused investment framework. For investors conditioned to "buy low, sell high" without regard to income streams, certain questions beg to be asked. The first is about valuation. Stock market investors are used to viewing the world through the simple and often singular lens of P/E ratios. P/Es may be useful in certain contexts, but they play a lesser role in a dividend-focused approach. The valuation metrics are based on the dividend yield, the growth of the dividend, and all the attendant ratios such as payout ratios of net income and free cashflow, capital intensity, working capital needs, etc. My "shorthand" equivalent to the stock market's P/E ratio is the Internal Rate of Return (IRR). It is the discount rate needed to make the future cashflows—dividend plus growth in the dividend—equal the current price. It is also the expected return on the investment. An IRR makes only one important assumption: a constant dividend growth figure in perpetuity. That is not realistic. But as long as the number is not too high, no more than nominal GDP growth over the past century or two, it is a reasonable shortcut, no less reasonable than the many assumptions built into P/E ratios. IRR has other virtues. It is an absolute metric, not a relative one, and it does not require the complicated math of risk-free rates, mysterious equity risk premia, and all the other legerdemain of modern finance. For businesspeople operating through the stock market, it is a simple and workable heuristic.

What level of IRR is attractive in this context? Higher is better, but a target of 4% or so yield and 4% or so dividend growth creates an expected nominal total return and nominal IRR of 8%. It is—above all else—reasonable. Depending on the portfolio and the investor, it can be a bit higher or a bit lower, but it is unheroic in its aspirations. Individual companies in the portfolio will have higher and lower IRRs, and their balance between current yield and future growth need not be exact. But at the portfolio level, having a balanced approach works well.

Note to P/E aficionados: Unless a company consistently has a payout ratio above 100% of net income, it is rather hard for the P/E of a high-dividend company to get to uncomfortable levels. Do the math. If a company has a 30 P/E and a 4% yield, it means they are paying out 120% of profits. That is not sustainable. It is much easier to have a very expensive and risky P/E of 40 with a 1% yield. In that case, the payout is just 40% of profits. But those are not dividend stocks. So keeping an eye on the yield and payout ratio is also a way to stay out of P/E trouble.

BUYBACKS AND VALUE INVESTING

Where are buybacks in this framework? Corporate share repurchase programs are a major part of the investment framework for the "buy low, sell high" stock market investor. They enjoy the semantic high ground as a key component of "cash returned to shareholders." Wall Street loves buyback announcements and all that they are supposed to represent. The shortcomings of buybacks have been addressed elsewhere in this account and in the academic literature. Suffice it here to say that they play almost no role in the investment framework for the business owner operating through the stock market. I say "almost" for two reasons. First, most large, publicly traded corporations that pay reasonable dividends also buy back their shares now and again, partially to offset share grants to employees and sometimes to retire shares issued as part of acquisitions. The former is simply compensation; the latter is a temporary capital structure adjustment. These might be considered more "environmental" buybacks as opposed to the very loud and visible "returning cash to shareholders" type.

There are rare instances when buybacks are an actual plus for the dividend investor. If management of a very high-yielding security has the cash to engage in a buyback, the effort may well serve to buttress the long-term dividend outlook for the remaining owners by mopping up dividend "leakage." Shares having an 8% yield that are canceled no longer have to make that payment. That may help secure the company's future distributions among a smaller number of company owners. These instances occur infrequently, usually during company-specific or market general sell-offs, when the yields become abnormally high. In those rare cases, buybacks can fit within a disciplined dividend investor's framework.

Being a dividend investor in a stock market means acknowledging the big difference between "value investing" as currently practiced and focusing on cash streams as a business owner.

While it is fair to observe that dividend investing is still a narrow subset of a broadly defined value exercise, the Venn diagram of the two now has only minimal overlap. At one time, the two disciplines were essentially identical—read your original Graham—but as dividends were stripped from the U.S. market, the value in value investing came to be based on other metrics. They include those "factors" common to the stock market such as low P/E and low P/B, and even multiples of EBITDA or some other internal, non-distributed cashflow measure, in either absolute or relative terms. (For a stock with material payouts, dividend yield might still be one of them.) There is certainly nothing wrong with buying and selling stocks on the basis of these factors. In fact, since the 1970s, factor investing has come to dominate the market, value being one of the two great investing styles (along with "growth"). But those characteristics say more about market participants' *opinions* about a company's condition and future than the reality already embedded in a dividend stream. That opinion imagines catalysts that will cause the value stock to "re-rate" and erase the current "mispricing." That is, the value investor is looking for something to change—perhaps dramatically. In contrast, the successful businessowner is focused on the continuation of current and future cashflows, not a "discovery" of the stock by other investors. It's more about the actual business than the stock market's view of the matter. Dividend investing is simply different.

INVESTMENT POLICY VERSUS TAX MINIMIZATION

Perhaps the biggest challenge to being a dividend investor in a stock market over the past two decades (beyond the limited opportunity set) has been the pushback in regard to taxes. That puzzles me. Differential tax rates involving dividend income and capital gains might have been a concern from the 1950s through the 1980s when the main tenets of modern academic finance were being worked out. But for the past two decades, the difference has been minimal. What has changed is that investors have had a choice to avoid dividend-paying stocks altogether. Starting in the 1990s and continuing to this day, payout ratios fell, the dividend yield of the market fell, and the number of major, leading corporations without dividends skyrocketed. The tax code has also allowed investors to minimize taxation of dividends by offering platforms—such as 401(k) programs and pension funds—where dividend payments are not directly taxed. The existence of these platforms permits allocation of distribution-rich holdings into the tax-deferred platforms while dividend-light and dividend-free stocks can be housed in directly taxed platforms such as brokerage accounts.

Still, even with that flexibility, let me state this boldly, and knowing full well that I will be pilloried by some financial advisors and investors: subordinating investment policy to tax strategy is a bad idea. There is certainly nothing wrong with minimizing taxation, but the question is "how far do you go out of your way to do so?" Recall our maxim in this investing enterprise, that minority shareholders in publicly traded entities should be laser-focused on the cash that they receive from their investments. Giving that up, just to avoid taxes, goes well beyond cutting off your nose to spite your face, or any other overreaction or self-defeating metaphor you prefer. It abandons the core purpose of investing, at least from my vantage point. But like many bad ideas, subordinating investment policy to tax strategy is common. In my day job, I see it all the time, which is a bit ironic because I oversee a dividend-focused strategy, which is all about delivering income in large amounts as frequently as possible to investors.

If tax minimization is an investor's overriding goal, they may want to consider municipal bonds. Yields there have been low in recent decades, but like the rest of the fixed-income market post-2022, cash returns from bonds are now back in a reasonable range. But the coupons don't grow the way that equity dividends can and generally do over time. Finally, the municipal bond market is around $4 trillion in size and not particularly liquid. Investors generally buy and hold to maturity. In contrast, the stock market as represented by the S&P 500 Index companies is quite liquid and worth $32 trillion at the end of 2022. There are lots of financial asset strategies that people can adopt to avoid taxation beyond municipal bond ownership. Sitting on the sidelines in cash is one option. But cash doesn't grow and is subject to purchasing power diminishment via inflation. Put the cash in a money market fund and inflation becomes less of a problem, but the income generated is generally taxable.

Within the stock market itself, another option is to avoid dividend-paying stocks entirely and just own non-dividend-paying stocks. In that instance, the investor pays taxes only when a capital gain is realized. Over the past few decades, this strategy has become very popular, and frankly very successful, because non-dividend-paying stocks have done so well. Bully for that strategy. Let's consider an extreme variant of that approach. The investor would hold not only non-dividend-paying stocks but also commodities, cryptocurrency, and other businesses that make no distributions. No distributions means no regularly recurring tax liability. A tax obligation would result only from the sale of an investment for a capital gain. The bad news should be obvious: the investor could lose every penny. Asset prices can and do go down, especially in that specific period when a harvested capital "gain" is needed to fund consumption.

So those are the options. While the harvested capital gains game has worked quite well over the past few decades, I still have to ask whether investors are willing to take on the risk of significant principal loss by ignoring companies that pay material dividends. In other words, playing the "capital gains only" game entails a great deal of risk. Is it more desirable to have an unrealized or realized loss than a taxable dividend payment? Somewhat surprisingly, there are apparently lots of investors who are okay with an unrealized loss rather than a taxable distribution. I'm not making a "federal case" out of this. I just want to point out some of the underappreciated implications of putting tax management ahead of investment strategy. In short, death and taxes may not be avoidable, but is it worth risking principal—potentially a lot of principal—to avoid incurring a known tax liability? No one wants to pay taxes, but it is a high-quality problem to have—a sign of success, not failure.

And it turns out the tax advantage of avoiding dividend-paying equities may not be worth it. In a recent assessment in the practitioner journal *The Journal of Wealth Management*, four AQR Capital Management investigators determined that, it turns out, avoiding dividend-paying securities just to avoid taxation of the coupons actually lowers pre-tax returns to a degree that it is not worth the effort (and somewhat unexpectedly lowers the ability to manage long-term capital gains). In short, "All things considered, the tax benefit of lowering the dividend yield is not enough to compensate for the associated increase in capital gains taxes and decrease in expected pre-tax returns."[4] Bending over backward to avoid dividends may be an example of being too clever by half. Wall Street excels at such stratagems and charges a pretty penny for them. If your goal is not paying taxes, you are not reading this book. If your goal is to maximize cashflow in a very conservative stock market investment strategy, do not subordinate investment policy to tax minimization.

PORTFOLIO CONSTRUCTION

Given the current market's scant regard for dividends, a critic will ask about portfolio construction. How can it be done in such a dividend-light market? Here, it is worth stepping back and understanding the point of Modern Portfolio Theory, to use diversification to achieve the optimal combination of expected total return and lowest possible standard deviation of total return. In practice, MPT has come to mean own everything and as much as you can, usually through index products. That would appear to challenge the dividend-focused investor in the U.S. stock market, where the options are more limited. It is only an appearance. Even in today's constrained environment, it is possible to achieve a reasonable balance of dividend yield and dividend growth through ownership of a well-diversified portfolio of real-economy companies. Here, it is also worth noting that because dividends do not jump around anywhere near as much as share prices, portfolio construction and measurement around a steady stream of high-and-rising dividends is mathematically less challenging than doing the same thing for share prices. In short, dividends offer the investor a smoother ride than the stock market's ever-gyrating motions. Ironically, in the math of Modern Portfolio Theory, it is quite possible to generate "alpha"—the holy grail of modern investment management—by lagging the market but doing so with such low volatility (standard deviation of total return) that the MPT statistics turn positive. That should tell you something about the usefulness of MPT. Dividend-oriented portfolio construction is discussed in greater detail in the final chapter of my earlier work, *Getting Back to Business*, from 2018.

***

The investment framework of dividend investing in a stock market might seem nonsensical in a low-inflation economy and with a market led ever higher by non-dividend payers of the type we've seen the past few decades. "Buy low, sell high" has worked quite well, with little if any regard to distributable cashflows to company owners. Dividend-focused investors have not participated in the high-octane share price appreciation of the non-dividend-paying securities during this period. The previous chapter outlined the rise of Nasdaq, its innovations, and its nearly dividend-free nature. There's no doubt about it. On a total return basis, low and non-div stocks have "shot the lights out" for the past 30 years. Dividends have mattered little for those investors content with capital gains—whether realized or unrealized—and undisturbed by the periodic collapse of the leading edge of the non-dividend stock universe, first during the internet bubble and more recently in 2022. The constancy, the cash-based returns, and the business-ownership basis of dividend-focused investing have just not mattered for many investors. That is fully acknowledged. But this framework has still worked for those investors who have sought material income and income growth from their assets, as well as very conservative stock market investors. Serving both of those constituencies has been my day job for the past two decades.

NOTES

[1] B Corporations are structured and operated to account for all stakeholders associated with an enterprise. Traditional corporations have a primary obligation to shareholders.

[2] Peris, *The Dividend Imperative*, 35–39.

[3] Median yields for the various cohorts are available at https://strategicdividendinvestor. com/the-ownership-dividend-charts-and-tables/.

[4] Ronen Israel, Joseph Liberman, Nathan Sosner, and Lixin Wang, "Should Taxable Investors Shun Dividends?", *The Journal of Wealth Management* (Winter 2019), 49–69. Quote from 49.

5

THE INVESTMENT INDUSTRY'S "TRUTH" VERSUS YOUR VERY PERSONAL "CLARITY"

Having outlined the investor relationship to stocks prior to the 1990s, and what has happened since, I now turn to why I think we are on the verge of a paradigm shift. This is where the "what's going to happen next" stage of the book would be if I were offering a quick fix to investors. Unfortunately, for those looking for instant riches, I am not that type of investor, analyst, or writer. Rather than names and dates, I want to start by providing something even more important: understanding and conviction. There is almost no practical discussion of investing in this chapter, but I genuinely believe that it is perhaps the most important part of this work. It is where, I hope, you determine your expectations and your approach to investing, where you set your priorities. Good books about investing are rarely about the narrow mechanics of buy, sell, and hold. They are, in one form or another, about decision-making. The academics have their view on the topic—which I covered in an earlier chapter—but that is less important

DOI: 10.4324/9781003292272-6

than properly framing the questions. So this chapter focuses on those questions. The answers will likely be unique to each investor. As is the case throughout this work, my approach is at odds with orthodox finance precepts and the decisions of the Nobel Prize Committee.

ASKING QUESTIONS ABOUT INVESTMENT TRUTH

Knowledge of the market may be a good thing, but self-knowledge is even better. It is what lets you sleep at night. Polonius may have been a long-winded fool, but his "to thine own self be true" was perhaps Shakespeare's best advice in regard to investing, and pretty much everything else. I'm sure that if you scrape through Ben Graham's work or Warren Buffett's commentaries, you can find a similar quote about self-knowledge. The timing for this exercise in self-knowledge—what I call here individual Clarity—could not be better. The last few years have been a head-scratching period from a stock market perspective, with rapid gyrations and major unanswered questions. Huge bets are being made, in opposite directions, on inflation, on interest rates, on earnings, on the market, on geopolitics, and on what follows three decades of the global neoliberal order. This period of transition makes it even more important, albeit harder, to know exactly what you want as an investor.

So let's start with a basic question, one you should ask yourself or get answered as part of your discussions with your financial advisor. What do you want from your stock market investing dollars? You'd think that it is a simple question and answer, but it really isn't. Is your goal a number, a certain level of assets that you are aiming for? That's certainly one option. Is it an expected amount of income on an annual or monthly basis to help you pay your bills? $3k a month, $5k a month? Is it a target date exercise, to have sufficient funds available at a particular time to purchase a property or pay for a child's or grandchild's education? Is it to have a total return of a certain percent annually, say 10% or 15%? Is it to beat the "market," and if so, how do you measure that? More subjectively, is it to have enough to retire to Florida, to sail around the world? Perhaps it is a combination of all of the above? Is it, to cite the old brokerage ad, "to be bullish on America," to own stakes in innovative companies, say social media or biotechs, without much worry about valuation or cashflow. That's a choice, too. At the other end of the spectrum, is your goal capital preservation only, to go with your distilled water, powdered milk, and gold bars in the basement? Is it perhaps a more general goal "to do well" and leave that undefined?

Or let's define the challenge in another way. Your investing goals may be whatever they are, but what about the risk you need to take to achieve them? Life involves risk; business involves risk; investing involves risk. When you speak to an investment advisor, he or she will mechanistically determine your risk level. Is it low, moderate, aggressive, etc.? How do you define those terms? Is it the risk of falling short of some goal, or the more serious risk of not meeting a critical need? Is it risk in terms of the income stream, in terms of the capital, in terms of the total return? Those are all different metrics. And over what time period are you considering the risk? When considering and measuring risk, timing matters. I have to look at share prices daily; you do not and should not. And are you using your definition of risk or someone else's? If you say you are considering risk (whatever definition) over a period of years, are you really?

Are you puzzled by all these questions? Surely, you are thinking, there is a simple and singular question and a simple and singular answer for both investment goals and the notion of risk. The investment industry has been around in an organized fashion for more than a century. About a half-century ago, it came up with a set answer. If you don't choose something for yourself, this is what you are going to get as an investment goal: the maximum amount of total return for a specific amount of risk, risk being defined as the standard deviation of total return. Or, if you flip that around, you get the lowest amount of risk for a given expected total return. It can be measured daily, but it usually is assessed on a monthly or a quarterly basis. Ideally, it should be viewed on a multi-year period. And those measurements are generally compared to a benchmark of some sort, a style-specific benchmark or a general market one such as the S&P 500 Index. It's what I call in this context investment Truth. It is officially sanctioned by the relevant authorities—academics and to some extent even regulators. Vast systems are designed to let you know where you stand versus this financial Holy Grail.

WHEN THE TRUTH JUST WON'T DO

For me to argue against this Truth—that is, focusing all your energy on maximizing risk-adjusted total return—could get me in trouble with the authorities, so I won't say that. What I can and will say is that very few investors actually follow the official prescription, perhaps because it is not particularly good advice. It's a one-size-fits-all handcuff, and it rarely if ever comports with what people actually want in life or from their investments. All the textbooks and all the training programs aim in this direction, and I'm not saying that it is not True—particularly in a classroom setting—but like many truths that people seek, it's a complicated, often-oversimplified quest.

This Truth falls short on many fronts. Even its inventor, Harry Markowitz, acknowledged that it was very hard to realize in practice. But for individual investors, it fails for easy-to-see answers. First, this goal is supposed to manifest itself over long measurement periods—no less than several years, and ideally longer. But most investors have much shorter time horizons. They say they are in the market for the long term and commit with their financial advisor for a particular strategy—whatever it may be—but the stock market appears to go against them for a few months, and they fold and change direction, usually at the wrong time, getting in at the top and out at the bottom of their particular strategy. This "near-termism" in investment timing is a well-known problem written about by many, including myself, but it cannot be mentioned enough.

In my case, as a manager of dividend-focused portfolios, it means having investors who swear they want income from their equities, who believe in dividend investing, who understand or say they understand the difference between investing for income and speculating in share prices, who sign on the bottom line, but … after a period in which non-dividend stocks did much better than dividend payers (2017–2021), they change their minds. They say they no longer need or want income; they just want to ride the electronic vehicle or biotech wave … *C'est la vie*. It's a free country, sort of, and the capital markets are open every day. If you want to change your goal in the market, that's fine. But let's not confuse that with investing. Or let's call it out as a very specific form of investing: chasing the hot dot, as we say, or a momentum strategy that invests in what is popular at the moment.

Think about it. Very few important decisions in life are taken lightly and then frequently reversed. Were the first few months of college or a new job or living in a new city easy? Probably not. Did you reverse course? Also probably not. But the stock market is open every day and lets you change direction, usually at great cost. Business investing the way I will be describing it is a long-term proposition and has the means—not a perfect mechanism—to sidestep the near-termism that is a plague to so many investors. Knowing what you want, stating it clearly, even if it is just to be a near-term speculator, is the key to not getting whipsawed around.

The second critical failing of the Truth is in regard to risk. Anyone who has even a passing familiarity with the stock market or any business venture understands that there is risk in any endeavor. And most stock market participants will acknowledge that there is some sort of risk involved. But how do you define risk? I know how I define it, and it has nothing to do with the standard deviation of total return over short or even intermediate measurement periods. But the greater problem is not the particular definition of risk. It's that most retail investors and plenty of institutional ones just want to beat the market in total return terms—mostly share price appreciation in short measurement periods. Period. That's their Truth. They show little concern for any definition of risk or actual risk in their analyses. They just want so-called outperformance last quarter, last year, every quarter, every year. There's nothing wrong with that at all. Aim high. As long as investors understand what they want and how it is measured, and most importantly, that they understand that their goal and their definition of risk—or utter disregard of risk—is a choice and that there are alternatives.

A variant of that theme is to give up entirely and just index the whole market and not even make an effort to choose goals or risks. Perhaps for some investors, that is their moment of Clarity. If so, that is fine. You are in good company, including Nobel Prize-winning economist James Tobin who argued in 1958 that individualized portfolios made no sense: just buy the market and toggle the amount of leverage or cash that you have. That was not a practical solution at the time, and it is not particularly practical now, but it is a justifiable approach to investing. However, it's not really business ownership through the stock market. And it can be extremely dangerous when only a handful of companies dominate the market, as is the case now. But if that is your Clarity, so be it. To summarize, having your goal be that stocks go up today (the popular variant) is vastly inferior to risk-adjusted total return over 3–5 years (the industry's stated but unobserved canonical Truth). And that Truth is itself inferior to your personal sleep-at-night investment Clarity.

CLARITY VERSUS TRUTH

So what do I mean by Clarity? Perhaps it is best to provide a few examples. They are subjective, necessarily, despite the efforts of the classical economists and finance professors over the past 60 years to frame all human choices in narrowly defined quantitative terms down to three decimal points. Those mechanical renderings of human decision-making can all-too-often lead to a false sense of precision and losing sight of the big picture. That big picture was captured by Kurt Vonnegut in 2005 when he penned a widely quoted appreciation for the *Catch-22* novelist, Joseph Heller. Vonnegut tells the story of Heller attending a billionaire's party on Shelter Island. Teased by Vonnegut about the billionaire's wealth, Heller responds:

> And Joe said, "I've got something he can never have."
> And I said, "What on earth could that be, Joe?"
> And Joe said, "The knowledge that I've got enough."

That's from *The New Yorker* issue of May 16, 2005. Its message is simple: Clarity.

Staying in the literary realm, you may be familiar with Tolstoy's folkloric short story, "How Much Land Does a Man Need?" If you are not, it is available in translation through your local bookstore. In it, a Russian peasant craving land invokes the devil, who offers him as much land as he can walk around in the course of one day, but he must return by sunset or he forfeits the land. The peasant charts a grand border before having to run back to his starting point at sunset. He arrives exhausted, only to collapse. His man-servant buries him in a six-foot grave. It turns out that was all that he needed.

A bit closer to our time and place, Christine Benz, Director of Personal Finance at Morningstar, has offered a stellar example of Clarity. She cites the "This I Believe" series on National Public Radio which is based on a similar radio show from the 1950s hosted by legendary newsman Edward R. Murrow. In the essays, prominent individuals discuss the core events and beliefs that have shaped their lives. As Benz writes,

> The series consistently demonstrates the value of having an overarching set of beliefs that can help you navigate tumultuous times. Think of your investment policy statement as your own, investment-related version of "This I Believe." In it, you'll articulate the key reasons why you're investing, what you're hoping to gain from your investments, whether you're on track to meet your goals, and whether any changes are in order. Once you've created one, you can use your investment policy statement as your compass, a check to keep your investment portfolio on course to meet its goals even when the market and your emotions are telling you to run for the hills. Referring to your investment policy statement before you make any investment decisions can help ensure that you're investing with your head, not your gut.[1]

This is an outstanding example of investment Clarity.

Market commentator and asset manager Barry Ritholtz has a similarly digestible version of Clarity. In a Bloomberg.com commentary from 2020,[2] he writes, and I summarize,

> You are not Warren Buffett [or Jim Simons or Bill Ackman or Howard Marks]. But here is the thing: You don't need to be. At least, you don't

> need to be any of these people in order to achieve the investment re-
> turns that will ensure a comfortable retirement. Your temperament is
> different from that of Munger or Simons or Buffett or Marks or whom-
> ever. We look at [the] fantastic wealth-creating trades [of these indi-
> viduals] and waste our time wondering, Why not me? Instead, find an
> investment style that suits your personality, available time and inter-
> ests as opposed to trying to match those with whom you have nothing
> in common ... Instead of trying to imitate the greats, understand your
> own personality.

In even fewer words, you have the great wisdom of George Goodman, writing as Adam Smith in the late 1960s: "If you don't know
who you are, the stock market is an expensive place to find out."[3]
It's not too difficult to find these types of statements from wise
market observers and participants. What's hard is making the
commitment to determining your personal Clarity, implementing
it, and sticking to it.

PERSONAL CLARITY

Few of us have the luxury of waxing poetic when it comes to our
finances or our retirement planning. That's the realm of cold hard
numbers, perhaps not the false precision of the finance professors,
but some combination of actual expectations tempered by personal
nature and unique circumstances. Let me give you an example of
where the two overlap. For whatever reason, I am a very conservative investor. Perhaps it is due to the fact that I am a historian and
have seen or studied too many bubbles burst through overly aggressive investing. Perhaps it is my thrifty grandparents—immigrants at
the turn of the last century—or my Depression-era parents. Whatever the cause, I've taken the stance that, as a minority investor in
publicly traded companies, I want a material income stream from
the enterprises to offset the agency cost of not being able (or particularly desiring) to run the companies myself. That has meant not
investing in those companies—such as the non-dividend-paying
market darlings and dominators over the past few decades—that
don't have material dividends. It's a choice that has meant giving
up relative total return. (In full disclosure, I did dabble in and write

about small, non-dividend-paying companies when I first made my way into financial research some 25 years ago. At the time, it was a necessary part of my job.) This approach is consistent with investments in real estate that I have made over the years. My wife and I own a handful of multi-family units. We bought the buildings, fixed them up, and rented them out. It is a cash-return business. There is little reason to view Verizon or Coca-Cola or Merck differently. In fact, because I control the former but have little meaningful say over the latter, there is even more reason to insist on a cash payment from the public equities.

The combination of cash yields and growth rates in the cash streams propelling the stocks I own higher over time has varied but in general has been in the high single digits. Since our real estate holdings are not for sale, the rate of return from the private assets is not directly visible, but the Internal Rate of Return has been in a similar high-single-digit range. That compares to low double-digit returns from the overall stock market—as measured by the S&P 500 Index—during the same time period. Juiced by very low interest rates, private equity assets have boasted higher double-digit returns for the past few decades. So, as of 2023 looking back in time, my investment returns goals have been below those offered by other risk opportunities. Why would I do that? Because I wanted to. As a starting premise, I insisted on a tangible cash investment stream and was willing to give up not having access to non-cash-paying investments. That might seem like a strange choice when everyone's goal is supposed to be maximizing return for a given amount of risk. Fans of Modern Portfolio Theory will chime in here that I just toggled my risk back and was content with lower returns. That's not the case. Instead, I started and maintained a commitment to having a tangible, cash nexus—whether in regard to stocks or private investments. The returns could have been lower or higher than the alternatives. For the past two decades, they have been modestly lower. We will see how they fare in the next few decades.

GETTING TO CLARITY

For me, having the investment be tangible was more important than catching the next unicorn. It was and remains a personal choice. What will be yours? To help you derive the answer, ask yourself the following subjective, philosophical questions. Are you a hedgehog—a person who anchors his or her decision-making on one big idea? Or are you a fox—who incorporates lots of inputs and changes course without regret? (I lean in the direction of hedgehog.) Do you aim for efficiency in your life, an option often leading to choices with the least involvement and least fees? Or do you prefer efficacy, an option leaning in the direction of engagement and customization? I lean in the direction of efficacy and can be content at the cost of some lost efficiency.

Your financial advisor's risk measurement software can get you only so far. Personal reflection is needed. More practically, ask yourself what you really want from your investing dollars, and what you are willing to put up with in order to achieve it. The behavioral finance gurus will tell you that your answers to the following questions might be wrong, but asking them is a necessary part of achieving investment Clarity. So, do you consider yourself tactical or strategic when it comes to investing? Are you patient or impatient? Are you easily distracted by the latest tidbit of news? Do you hover over the stock market day and night, or pay little attention to the market? Are you able to admit what you are good at, and what you are not good at, when it comes to designing and implementing a financial plan? What gives you pleasure or pain in investing? Is it a dividend announcement or a "pop" in the stock? Or a quarterly "miss"? Do you have strong views, or any views, about the direction of the economy, the market, or valuations? Some non-financial questions are equally important: How well do you know your financial advisor? Do they understand how to align a portfolio with your personality? As you work out your plan, make sure to consult someone who has that capability.

Your individual Clarity will likely come not from a brief moment of reflection. It will probably take a while to be worked out. Better start now. How will you know when you have achieved investing Clarity? Sleeping well at night without agonizing over your finances excessively is probably one sign. Having it be consistent with your personality á la Barry Ritholtz is another. Once your investments are lined up in that manner, you will be unlikely to zig and zag in your investment choices. You will be able to tolerate near-term setbacks without undue anxiety. And you probably won't be checking the market every single day. Once you have come to your version of Clarity, the rest of your investment decisions flow naturally. The actual investments may work out, or not, but the logic is consistent. And it is not the specific investment choices that you make that matter—to be a high-octane biotech IPO investor, to limit yourself to leveraged private equity ventures, to focus on real estate, or pizza delivery franchises, or to want maximum total return, or to play it safe with gold in the basement or by buying an all-market ETF and never looking again, whatever. Those are all fine choices. The point is that you decide, understand, and accept the consequences of your decision.

***

So it is in life, so it is in investing. Once you have a clearly defined framework—Clarity—your decisions will make sense because they fit within the intellectual framework set out in the beginning. Without that framework, you run the risk of drifting, without rudder or anchor, dabbling in this, dabbling in that, knowing not what to do, and generally being unhappy about it. The great weakness of modern finance is that it pretends to have solved the challenge of decision-making under conditions of uncertainty. It has replaced unquantifiable, all-too-human uncertainty with quantifiable, all-too-calculated risk. And it purportedly allows you to choose your desired outcome of expected risk and return. That is a bridge too far. Let us be more humble in our presumed mastery of the human condition.

NOTES

[1] www.morningstar.com/articles/619888/making-your-investment-policy-statement, originally published in 2013.
[2] www.bloomberg.com/opinion/articles/2020-04-24/why-you-re-not-one-of-the-world-s-great-investors?sref=vBm6bz3t, originally published in 2020.
[3] George Goodman, "Adam Smith," in *The Money Game* (New York: Random House, 1968).

6

AN ACADEMIC REBUTTAL

While Wall Street has had no time for dividends in recent decades and has had the support of much of academia in that regard, it has not had complete cover. Given my expectation that a cash-based relationship between minority owners and companies is likely to return to greater prominence in the decades ahead, it is worth noting the "resistance" of those academics who found the cash-based relationship to be the norm. I've already covered the commentaries of Irving Fisher, John Burr Williams, and the practitioner work of Ben Graham, all of which assumed a full and natural cash-based investing framework. But there is much more. As we head again toward that type of environment, it is worth revisiting the academic literature supportive of investing in a businesslike manner.

THE LINTNER DIVIDEND CANON

The broad-based academic study of large corporations occurred only after World War II, in parallel with the rise of academic finance in general. Five years before M&M declared dividend

DOI: 10.4324/9781003292272-7

payout policy irrelevant, Harvard Professor John Lintner took dividend policy very seriously. In an article in the high-profile *American Economic Review* in 1956, Lintner concluded that stability of payouts mattered a great deal to both investors and corporate managers.[1] Current earnings and recent payouts were viewed as significant factors. That's not revolutionary now, but it needed to be said somewhere, by somebody, first. And so it was. In the business analysis literature, Lintner's study has the same "foundational" status as M&M's article does among what I call the "anti-dividend" community.

Most if not all of the academic accounts referenced here that focus on a company's dividend policy mention Lintner as a starting point for the analysis of dividend policies. Lintner's analysis was necessarily data-poor. Since then, academics have been updating Lintner's model with new data, new factors, and new interpretations as to what drives dividend policy. As an example, you can pick up a scintillating copy of John Brittain's *Corporate Dividend Policy*, a tome published by the Brookings Institution in 1966. It starts with an observation justifying the study that still stands today: "Since profits are less reliably measured than dividends, the behavior of the latter alone is … worth noting."[2] Yes, indeed. Other observers have made that accounting point in favor of dividends more explicitly. In a bolder fashion, Peter Bernstein wrote that

> (w)ith the best of intentions, the earnings that accountants and managers report with such precision ("We earned $2.01 this quarter versus $1.96 last year") are nothing more than estimates, with built-in vulnerabilities. Nobody knows how to measure true earnings. Everybody knows the precise amount of a dividend declaration.[3]

The general Lintner line of academic analysis continues to this day, usually referring to him, sometimes not.[4] Importantly, the modernization of Lintner over the past several decades has necessarily included an analysis of share repurchases as one of the management options. The common factor in all of them is that they take dividend payouts as a serious subject of business analysis. In the shadow of the M&M's assertion that payout ratios don't matter, the very existence of this large Lintner literature raises the question

of the M&M propositions' relevance, at least in their more extreme application that goes beyond the payout ratio to the dividends themselves.

And it is worth noting that almost all of these Lintner commentaries were or are quite aware of the tax penalty, for both corporations and investors (since 1954), of dividend payments. But they
are not dismissive of the concept of sharing profits of an enterprise, even if it is disadvantageously taxed. And they do not auto-
matically assume that a harvested capital gain is naturally superior,
or even comparable to a profit distribution.

Not surprisingly, successful business leaders also continue to
consider what their appropriate dividend payout ought to be, á
la Lintner's question from over 60 years ago or Alfred Sloan from
even earlier, or the directors of the Dutch East India Company
four centuries ago. In my role as a portfolio manager, I speak to
company management teams all the time as they consider the
right level of dividends, given their profits, their investment requirements, their business prospects, and investor expectations.
This is much in line with the spirit of Lintner's original analysis
from 1956. Many of these business leaders have their MBAs from
the University of Chicago, have heard of M&M, and understand
behavioral finance. And yet nevertheless, to borrow a metaphor
from another area of struggle, they "persist." Perhaps they persist
in paying dividends and considering the appropriate payout level
for their companies because that exercise is in the very nature of
business ownership and management.

DIRECTLY CHALLENGING M&M

The extensive Lintner literature is an implicit diminishment of
the M&M irrelevance proposition, but few academics appear to
want to take on the Nobel laureates directly. There are exceptions,
including a husband-and-wife economist team, Harry and Linda
DeAngelo. Their "Irrelevance of the MM Dividend Irrelevance
Theorem," from 2005, is available on SSRN.[5] In it, the DeAngelos
unwind the M&M assumption that all firms would have large
capital expenditure requirements and would therefore be reliant
on external financing. The DeAngelos note that most firms now

can get by on internal financing—the exception that M&M called "treacherous," as discussed in Chapter 2. Once the handcuffing restriction of external financing is removed, dividend policy and investment policy are set free. There can be an optimal ratio of one to the other. M&M no longer applies.

The DeAngelos continue and highlight, as I have, that too many managers go beyond what M&M actually wrote—about payout policy under perfect conditions not changing the market value of the firm—to a separate and total disregard of dividends themselves. So instead of a dividend fallacy, those managers labor under a non-dividend fallacy. They write,

> some signs indicate that the polar opposite fallacy—that managers can totally ignore payout policy—has now taken root ... Specifically, Brav ... finds that 58.4% of CFOs of firms that have neither paid dividends nor repurchased stock (in the last three years) indicate that their firms may never pay dividends or repurchase stock. It is possible that many survey respondents expect their firms to be acquired or to go bankrupt before paying dividends or buying back stock, or that they misunderstood the question. ... But it is also possible that some (or even many) finance officers of major corporations believe that payout policy is irrelevant in the sense that firms can permanently avoid all payouts.[6]

In the present paradigm, management teams can get away with a cavalier attitude toward the cash nexus; in the upcoming one, they will not have that luxury.

DIVIDENDS VERY MUCH MATTER

As welcome as the DeAngelo revolt against M&M is, and as helpful and illuminating as the Lintner payout ratio literature is, these pushbacks were and are rather narrow. Just looking at payout ratios and the various factors that contribute to them is not the same thing as asserting the centrality of distributable cashflows to the business ownership and valuation process. Fortunately, that perspective was taken up just about the time that the Lintner literature was appearing. John Burr Williams had initially tried to do so in the 1930s, and it is implied in the work of Benjamin Graham in the same period. But two decades later, Myron Gordon, James Walter, and Ezra Solomon grabbed John Burr Williams by the scruff of the neck and brought him into the realm of modern academic finance, linking the valuation of companies to their dividend. Gordon gave his name to a simple formula, the Gordon Dividend Growth model, which is a neat trick for deriving a reasonable price for a security based on its current yield, its forecast dividend growth rate, and a discount rate. Alternatively, it can be used to forecast an expected rate of return as the simple addition of the current yield and the dividend growth rate. Like all simple formulas, it takes shortcuts but is helpful as part of a broader set of valuation and portfolio management tools.[7]

The works of Gordon, Walter, and Solomon are dated in language and details, but they are worth recalling because they are crystal clear and relevant in one regard: the value of an asset is directly linked to the present value of what you, the minority shareholder, can expect to get from it in cash over time. Period. And that literature was equally clear in asserting that a dollar dividend now was more highly appreciated by investors than the prospect of an equal or even greater amount of capital appreciation at some point in the future. As Solomon wrote,

> it may be due to a general lack of faith in the market's ability to prevent wide prolonged departures of realizable market value from intrinsic values and hence to a preference for a stable dividend policy that does not require an investor to sell part of his holdings in each period for income purposes. ... In an uncertain world in which verbal statements can be ignored or misinterpreted, dividend action does provide a clear-cut means of "making a statement" that speaks louder than a thousand words.[8]

This cash-focused literature was subsequently dismissed by the soon-to-be-prevailing efficient market orthodoxy in academic finance as the "bird in the hand" fallacy. That still dominant school of thought rejects the idea that a dollar dividend in hand is worth more than the prospect of some greater amount in capital appreciation down the road due to successful reinvestment by management and the resulting share price gains. Modern finance much prefers the 2 or 20 or 200 birds that might be hiding in the bushes. That's fine; that's a choice. But the cash dividend in hand will and does have a meaningful attraction to many investors.

Now to be fair, fortune has favored the bold over the past several decades, with only periodic setbacks. Despite those momentary drawdowns, the bush has turned out to hold many a quail and grouse, with a decline in the market yield (the bird in the hand) and the substantial capital appreciation of the non-dividend payers (the many in the bush). So bully for the hunters. But the choice is not without risk. As one of the other 1950s authors put it clearly,

> A higher proportion of earnings retained [that is, a lower dividend pay-out ratio] is associated with greater price appreciation. The crucial factor is the profitable utilization of investors' funds. The studies of the individual companies demonstrate that the mere fact of low dividend payout does not guarantee outstanding price appreciation. Increases in earning power must accompany the increases in book value arising from undistributed profits if price appreciation is to be enjoyed.[9]

In short, management must invest those undistributed profits very well if the math is to work out. It is the same challenge in 2023 as it was in 1953. And whatever has been the case for the past 70 years, what of the next 30? Will it be like the last few decades, or will it revert to the standards of business observable in the private and public markets around the globe and throughout recorded history other than the Nasdaq phenomenon?

DIVIDENDS AND AGENCY

While the observations of Gordon et al. were very helpful from a valuation perspective, they did not and still do not constitute a specific theory of investment based, on the one hand, the separation of management from ownership and, on the other, the natural distribution of profits above investment needs to company owners. An important step in that direction came two decades later when Michael C. Jensen, writing with William H. Meckling, created a proto-theory of the firm built around the idea of agency costs.[10] An agency cost is when you get someone to do something for you that you can't or just don't want to do yourself. For example, say, create, fund, and manage entirely the Coca-Cola Corporation. So you have someone else do that on your behalf. At a simpler level, you may or may not mow your own lawn. There's a trade-off involved in doing it yourself versus having someone else do it. Fewer people do their own dentistry; most go to a third person to handle that task. But the agent or agents do so at a cost, not just a cash cost—which is obvious—but a cost associated with differences of opinion, imagination, and execution. In this context, the modern corporation is a way of getting big things done, but getting them done somewhat imperfectly from the perspective of a minority shareholder.

Berle & Means in 1932 had earlier framed the distinctive element of modern corporations as being this separation of ownership and management. They were mostly interested in the general and legal issues, not costs and cashflows. In contrast, Jensen focused on costs and cashflows. He understood modern corporations through the prism of these agency costs. Jensen was not the first to see this problem. He starts his article with a well-known extended quote from Adam Smith, writing two centuries earlier in the age of the earliest joint-stock companies. It perfectly distills what Jensen would elaborate on two centuries later:

> The directors of such [joint-stock] companies, however, being the managers rather of other people's money than of their own, it cannot well be expected, that they should watch over it with the same anxious vigilance with which the partners in a private co-partnery frequently watch over their own. Like the stewards of a rich man, they are apt to consider attention to small matters as not for their master's honour, and very easily give themselves a dispensation from having it. Negligence and profusion, therefore, must always prevail, more or less, in the management of the affairs of such a company.[11]

Jensen did not pass judgment the way that Smith did. In fact, Jensen justified the costs as unavoidable if you—as we all do—wish to invest above and beyond our means to entirely control an enterprise. That is, if all you wish to do is run the pizza parlor, you can control it entirely. But if you wish to go beyond the small enterprise, you have to make compromises. Agency costs cannot be avoided; the alternative is to stick to the small family business. Jensen concludes ebulliently and quite at odds with Berle & Means:

> The publicly held business corporation is an awesome social invention. Millions of individuals voluntarily entrust billions of dollars, francs, pesos, etc., of personal wealth to the care of managers on the basis of a complex set of contracting relationships which delineate the rights of the parties involved. The growth in the use of the corporate form as well as the growth in market value of established corporations suggests that at least, up to the present, creditors and investors have by and large not been disappointed with the results, despite the agency costs inherent in the corporate form. ... Moreover, there were alternative organizational forms available, and opportunities to invent new ones. Whatever its shortcomings, the corporation has thus far survived the market test against potential alternatives.[12]

A decade later, in 1986, Jensen elaborated on his agency theory of the firm specifically from the perspective of cashflows and their dispositions.[13] In it, he created a new framework for considering the minority shareholder. In short, he asked, "who controls the cash?" He answered:

> Corporate managers are the agents of shareholders, a relationship fraught with conflicting interests. The payout of cash to shareholders creates major conflicts that have received little attention. Payouts to shareholders reduce the resources under managers' control, thereby reducing managers' power, and making it more likely they will incur the monitoring of the capital markets. ... Conflicts of interest between shareholders and managers over payout policies are especially severe when the organization generates substantial free cash flow. The problem is how to motivate managers to disgorge the cash rather than investing it at below the cost of capital or wasting it on organization inefficiencies.[14]

Jensen sees higher payouts as a means of managing these conflicts, but he isn't really a dividend guy. Indeed, in the remainder of his

1986 article, Jensen goes down a separate rabbit hole involving debt and acquisitions. But the great financial journalist and advisor Peter Bernstein took Jensen's argument to an extreme, at least for the purposes of discussion. In a polemic from 2005, he suggested, strikingly, that companies should be forced to pay out 100% of their free cashflow and go to the discriminating and judgmental stock market whenever they needed new investment capital. He wrote, "A world of mandated 100 percent payouts, in which any expenditure of the stockholders' money beyond current operating expenses would have to meet the test of the capital markets, would exhibit no empire building, no cash hoarding, no unnecessary diversification."[15] It's a provocative assertion, and one that, ironically, would validate M&M's proposition. I'm not certain that I'm in favor but I'm delighted to see someone, even if tongue in cheek, propose the opposite to the idiotic zero payout policy that investors have had to encounter so frequently in the current paradigm.

Jensen creates a useful way for minority shareholders to think about their investments. As a public company investor of several decades standing, I do see the main challenge to being a dividend investor in a stock market in these terms. Yes, we trust management; yes, they are very good at their jobs; but no, we do not give them a blank check all the time. The dividend forces them to have to make decisions even more rigorously than they might otherwise wish to. As a minority shareholder with no direct control over the operations of the company, this is what I want, even if it comes at a cost of some missed growth opportunities.

More broadly, Jensen's agency cost model can describe the entire process of investing through the modern asset management industry. It is a sequence of cash costs, preferences, differences of opinions, variety of competencies, and even personalities. They start with the investor, continue to the financial advisor, then to the various levels of the distribution firm, then the asset manager, and then to the chosen investments. Those investments—in this case stocks—have their board of directors, their executives, line employees, etc. But the challenge is the same. You like the idea, you like the business, you like the prospects, and you can live with the valuation, but there will always be frictions in implementing the strategy and realizing the profits. Like Lintner, Michael Jensen spawned an entire literature on financial agency costs. You don't have to read it. The point is to know that it exists, and that one can use the language of agency theory to understand the headwinds and tailwinds that one encounters as a minority shareholder of a publicly traded corporation.

SIGNALING

Similar in time and nature to agency theory is another partial answer to the dividend puzzle, that is, signaling theory. It's not that hard to see a dividend as a signal from company management to investors about the prospects for the company. First, the management has asymmetric, "inside"—not illegal, just inside—information (and judgment) that, as a practical matter, investors cannot have. Remember again the separation of ownership and management in the modern corporation. So management signals how things are going through setting the dividend. À la Lintner, they smooth it in light of recent payments, raise it when they see very good times ahead, and lower it when the opposite is true.

But how good of a signal is it? And what about other ways to convey information—earnings releases, press releases, forward guidance, conference calls, conference presentations, etc.? Well, none of those mechanisms involve cold hard cash. They are just words. And the numbers that are on a financial release aren't much better. A theory formalizing this signaling notion in regard to dividends was offered in 1979 by Sudipto Bhattacharya.[16] There is now a whole school of academic literature on dividend signaling. It's mostly negative. I readily admit that. That is, the finance professors can't really find much of a meaningful correlation between the signal and future outcomes, in terms of either share prices or future dividends. Perhaps, but using a bit of agency theory, we conclude that our agents in the corporation, the senior executives, are not clairvoyant. They are pretty good at signaling about the past and only mediocre about the future, just like the rest of us. That's a shame, but it's probably true. The world is messy. Management signaling prospective business conditions through the dividend is just one of many tools the investor has at his or her disposal. Signaling may not be perfect, but it is part of the overall analytical mosaic for the business investor operating in the stock market.

WHY DIVIDENDS STILL MATTER

That mosaic has been put together in the academy by none other than the DeAngelos and their co-author Douglas Skinner, now a dean at the University of Chicago School of Business. Their "Corporate Payout Policy" from 2008 is a mashup of the prior academic work but will certainly do at the practitioner level as an explanation and justification from the academy for companies paying dividends and investors seeking them out. So at last we have an answer for the M&M-based dismissal of dividends, and it is nearly as mellifluous: M&M, meet D&D. I need to work their co-author Douglas Skinner into the acronym. DDS is the name for a dentist's academic degree. I'm not certain that's the way to go. For now, however, DDS

> conclude that a simple asymmetric information framework that empha-
> sizes the need to distribute FCF and that embeds agency costs (as in
> Jensen, 1986) and security valuation problems (as in Myers and Majluf,
> 1984) does a good job of explaining the main features of observed pay-
> out policies—i.e., the massive size of corporate payouts, their timing
> and, to a lesser degree, their (dividend versus stock repurchase) form.[17]

Importantly, the authors show their hand clearly in their first chapter heading: "Basic Theory: The Need to Distribute FCF Is Foundational." That puts them very much at odds with current practice in corporate America and on Wall Street.

DDS directly addresses the supposed tax advantage of share re-purchases over dividends, noting that the tax argument fails on the logic test because share repurchases took off after the tax rates were essentially equalized:

> Although academics almost always cite the tax advantages of repur-
> chases as the reason for why the survival of dividends is a puzzle, a
> reasonable case can be made that taxes are not a first-order determi-
> nant of the choice between the two forms of payout. As Grinblatt and

> Titman ... point out, tax law changes in 1982 and 1986 "substantially decreased the tax disadvantage of dividends," thus should have encouraged firms to substitute out of stock repurchases and into dividends. Yet exactly the opposite occurred, with the repurchase boom beginning in the 1980s.[18]

So, if we finally have an answer to the "dividend puzzle" that has so long confounded so many academics, a fair question is why M&M, Fischer Black, and the "dividend fallacy" behavioralists are so much better known than Lintner & DDS among the practitioner community. Well, I don't know. Maybe they are smarter. They have a lot more Nobel Prizes in economics. Miller & Modigliani each have one. And they were both part of coming up with much bigger parts of modern finance. On the other side of the equation, Lintner, Jensen, and the others have lots of citations, but no trips to Stockholm. Jensen probably should have. Only Robert Shiller, a Yale economist who took dividends seriously (in work from the 1980s) but does not focus on them, has the blessing of the Nobel committee.

I have a different explanation. The anti-dividend crowd is quite normative—their work is about how the world should be—in perfect markets, with perfectly rational investors, unlimited growth opportunities, perfect management foresight, and as few real-world considerations as possible, all occurring in a broad economic system in equilibrium, explained in mostly simple formulas. For the "dividend fallacy" folks, on the other hand, all of the investor mistakes are departures from a still-assumed "norm" of profit maximizing, rational actors operating in a chalkboard economy. They are the exceptions that prove the rule, so to speak. In setting such a high bar for human behavior, academic finance is trying to mimic the hard sciences; it has physics envy.[19] It tries to get human behavior in all of its complexity reduced to a series of equations. As a result, academic finance models are often far too constrained. The only way they can be made "scientific" is by rendering human behavior unrealistic and often misleading when applied to the world as it is. The academic sentiment against dividend investing still reflects this 1960s-era pendulum swing far away from the actual world toward an idealized one. Some humility and some real-world business experience by academics might go a long way toward having the pendulum return from that extreme.

In contrast, the Lintner and Jensen schools describe the world as it is: messy, not easily mathematical. In that world, culture matters. In that world, history matters. Here you can see my bias as a historian. Some financial economists are willing to adopt a similar view, probably at the risk of incurring the wrath of their colleagues. George Frankfurter and Bob Wood summarized their research into the history of dividend analysis and concluded that

> [a]ll academic models [since the 1950s] have been developed in the tradition of neoclassical economics, with the underlying assumption that dividend payments to shareholders have a pure economic pretense. [In contrast], our conclusion ... is that dividend-payment patterns (or what is often referred to as "dividend policy") of firms are a cultural phenomenon, influenced by customs, beliefs, regulations, public opinion, perceptions and hysteria, general economic conditions and several other factors, all in perpetual change, impacting different firms differently. Accordingly, it cannot be modeled mathematically and uniformly for all firms at all times.[20]

Dividends remain popular, they argue, because they were paid from the earliest joint-stock companies and then paid for three centuries before the most vocal academics determined that the only valid approach to stock investing is asset price-based, not cashflow-based. I may not agree with all Frankfurter & Wood's assertions, but I do appreciate their historical approach.

***

While most investors could not care less whether the academics are for or against them, for those investors who take comfort in knowing that there is an intellectual framework behind their practitioner efforts, the work of Lintner and his heirs is welcome. Even for those investors, the dividend-centric approach may seem like a dated technology compared to the new shiny objects that Wall Street produces on a regular basis. In the next chapter, I will argue why that view is incorrect. History does not repeat itself, but it is a very helpful guide. And after the last 30 years of unusual capital market characteristics, investors will likely see a reversion to age-tested practices over the next few decades.

NOTES

[1] John Lintner, "Distribution of Incomes of Corporations Among Dividends, Retained Earnings, and Taxes," *The American Economic Review*, Vol. 46, no. 2 (May 1956), 97–113. There is also the parallel study of business factors contributing to dividend policy in Paul G. Darling, "The Influence of Expectations and Liquidity on Dividend Policy," *Journal of Political Economy*, Vol. 65, no. 3 (June 1957), 209–224. Among the many works fine tuning the work of Lintner, see John A. Brittain, *Corporate Dividend Policy* (Washington, DC: Brookings Institution, 1966); Eugene F. Fama and Harvey Babiak, "Dividend Policy: An Empirical Analysis," *Journal of the American Statistical Association*, Vol. 63, no. 324 (December 1968), 1132–1161. Lintner's survey was subsequently updated in H. Kent Baker, Gail E. Farrelly, and Richard B. Edelman, "A Survey of Management Views on Dividend Policy," *Financial Management*, Vol. 14, no. 3 (Autumn 1985), 78–84. Importantly for our purposes, the authors of that latter study noted that "respondents from all three industry groups thought that investors have different perceptions of the relative riskiness of dividends and retained earnings and hence are not indifferent between dividend and capital gain returns." (82) That's a direct, practitioner, business manager repudiation of a central tenet of orthodox finance in regard to dividends. Baker continued to update the survey work 15 years later: H. Kent Baker and Gary E. Powell, "Determinants of Corporate Dividend Policy: A Survey of NYSE Firms," *Financial Practice and Education*, Vol. 10, no. 4 (2000), 29–40.

[2] John A. Brittain, *Corporate Dividend Policy* (Washington, DC: Brookings Institution, 1966), 2–3.

[3] Peter L. Bernstein, "Dividends and the Frozen Orange Juice Syndrome," *Financial Analysts Journal*, Vol. 61, no. 2 (March–April 2005), 26.

[4] For a survey of that literature see, Franklin Allen and Roni Michaely, "Payout Policy," in G.M. Constantinides, M. Harris, and R. Stulz, eds. *Handbook of the Economics of Finance*, Vol. 1 (Amsterdam: Elsevier, 2003), 339–422. See also Alon Brav, John R. Graham, Campbell R. Harvey, and Roni Michaely, "Payout Policy in the 21st Century," *Journal of Financial Economics*, Vol. 77 (2005), 483–527. This account is an explicit update to Lintner and finds that share repurchases have joined dividend payouts as the central topic of the interviews.

[5] Harry DeAngelo and Linda DeAngelo, "The Irrelevance of the MM Dividend Irrelevance Theory," SSRN 680855 (2005). It was published the following year as Harry DeAngelo and Linda DeAngelo, "The Irrelevance of the MM Dividend Irrelevance Theorem," *Journal of Financial Economics* (February 2006), 293–315. I have not been able to review that version.

[6] H. DeAngelo, L. DeAngelo, and D. J. Skinner, "Corporate Payout Policy," *Foundations and Trends in Finance*, Vol. 3, nos. 2–3 (2008), 95–287, quote from 109.

[7] Among the articles in this set, see Myron J. Gordon and Eli Shapiro, "Capital Equipment Analysis: The Required Rate of Profit," *Management Science*, Vol. 3, no. 1 (October 1956), 102–110; James E. Walter, "Dividend Policies and Common Stock Prices," *The Journal of Finance*, Vol. 11, no. 1 (March 1956), 29–41; Ezra Solomon, *The Theory of Financial Management* (New York: Columbia University Press, 1963); Myron J. Gordon, "Dividends, Earnings and Stock Prices," *The Review of Economics and Statistics*, Vol. 44 (1963), 99–105. Prior work in this direction was made by Oscar Harkavy, "The Relation Between Retained Earnings and Common Stock Price for Large, Listed Corporations," *The Journal of Finance*, Vol. 8, no. 3 (September 1953), 283–297.

8 Solomon, *The Theory of Financial Management*, 142.

9 Harkavy, "The Relation Between... .", 297.

10 Michael C. Jensen and William H. Meckling, "Theory of the Firm: Managerial Behavior, Agency Costs and Ownership Structure," *Journal of Financial Economics*, Vol. 3 (1976), 305–360.

11 Adam Smith, *The Wealth of Nations*, 1776, Cannan Edition (New York: Modern Library, 1937), 700.

12 Jensen and Meckling, "Theory of the Firm," 357.

13 Michael C. Jensen, "Agency Costs of Free Cash Flow, Corporate Finance, and Takeovers," *The American Economic Review*, Vol. 76, no. 2 (May 1986), 323–329.

14 Jensen, "Agency Costs of Free Cash Flow," 323.

15 Bernstein, "Dividends and the Frozen Orange Juice Syndrome," 28.

16 Sudipto Bhattacharya, "Imperfect Information, Dividend Policy, and 'the Bird in the Hand' Fallacy," *The Bell Journal of Economics* (Spring 1979), 259–270; John Kose and Joseph Williams, "Dividends, Dilution, and Taxes: A Signaling Equilibrium," *Journal of Finance*, Vol. 40, no. 4 (September 1985), 1053–1070; Merton Miller and K. Rock, "Dividend Policy Under Asymmetric Information," *Journal of Finance* (September 1985), 1031–1051; Frank Easterbrook, "Two Agency-Cost Explanations of Dividends," *American Economic Review*, Vol. 74, no. 4 (September 1984), 650–659; David J. Denis, Diane K. Denis and Atulya Sarin, "The Information Content of Dividend Changes: Cash Flow Signaling, Overinvestment and Dividend Clienteles," *The Journal of Financial and Quantitative Analysis*, Vol. 29, no. 4 (December 1994), 567–587.

17 Harry DeAngelo, Linda DeAngelo, and Douglas Skinner, "Corporate Payout Policy," *Foundations and Trends in Finance*, Vol. 3, nos. 2–3 (2008), 95–287; initial quote from 95.

18 DeAngelo, DeAngelo, and Skinner, "Corporate Payout Policy," 236.

19 For an overview of that envy, see James Owen Weatherall, *The Physics of Wall Street: A Brief History of Predicting the Unpredictable* (New York: Houghton, Mifflin, Harcourt, 2013).

20 George M. Frankfurter and Bob G. Wood, Jr., "The Evolution of Corporate Dividend Policy," *Journal of Financial Education*, Vol. 23 (Spring 1997), 16–33, quote from 31.

7

A NEW INVESTING REALITY

The 40-year decline in interest rates has come to an end. That's the tweet. Even by the nano-second attention span of most market participants, it is a short summary. But it packs a wallop, because it essentially reverses, or at least halts, several capital market trends that have dominated the investing landscape for the past three decades. The likely consequences of this trend ending are outlined in this chapter. It's doubtful that all of them will be realized in full measure, but after three full decades of nearly anything goes in the stock market, the pendulum will be swinging back toward more normal business relationships. Please note that this is not a call for higher-for-longer interest rates. For ushering in the changes outlined in this work, it is sufficient just for interest rates to no longer persistently decline.

CASH COMPETITION FOR CAPITAL

The first and perhaps most important aspect of the "return to normal" will be the competition for capital. Investors may have

DOI: 10.4324/9781003292272-8

wildly varying styles, goals, and preferences, but they agree on one thing: financial markets are a platform for competition. That competition can take various forms, but the most obvious one is for a cash rate of return. Yet, decades of declining interest rates have distorted capital allocation. Now that money once again costs something and risk (however defined) is a positive number, that battle for your investment dollars should become less distorted over time. For instance, cash itself (in the form of short-term government securities and money market funds) now has a positive return. It's not much, 4%–5% or so as of mid-2023, but that is infinitely above the minimal compensation for cash that investors have received over much of the last decade. On the other hand, bond prices have benefitted from 40 years of declining rates. Now that rates have stopped going down—and as of mid-2023 are at more typical absolute levels—that tailwind is gone. And after the sharp correction in 2022 and 2023, bonds again have meaningful yields in the mid-single-digit range. That may make them attractive once again, but it will have to be on merits of the coupon and the credit, not an expectation of sustained rate declines pushing up their values.

The pressure for higher cash returns will not be limited to publicly traded assets. More than a decade of nearly cashless capital markets gave much greater prominence to types of assets which, under normal circumstances, would have been niche products at best. Yes, private equity and venture capital and "alternatives" of all stripes existed prior to the decline in rates. But the super-oxygenated air of the low-rate period allowed these asset classes to take flight and find their way into Main Street portfolios. As I write in mid-2023, crypto has stumbled and private equity is whistling past the cemetery before they have to mark their holdings to genuine values. Asset allocation is due for a comeuppance. The mantra of diversifying into ever more exotic investment vehicles should never have been particularly relevant to Main Street investors due to lack of scale, liquidity, costs, and returns, but it took the rise in risk rates to pop that bubble. And those are the serious "alts." The SPACs, NFTs, and unicorns do not even warrant mention. Rising risk rates have chased them from the investment stage.

STOCK PAYOUTS AND YIELDS

The question is what equities will look like in this new environment. While the stock market sold off sharply in 2022, the cash yield represented by the S&P 500 Index ended the year still well less than 2%. In a low and declining interest rate environment, the cash return of equities mattered less and less. Now it will matter more and more. Entering into this new period, 103 S&P 500 Index companies had zero dividends (as of 12/31/2022). Another 66 had yields below 1%. A further 114 had yields between 1% and 2%—which I still consider to be immaterial. That is, the U.S. stock market at the aggregate level is ill-prepared to compete on a cash basis for capital. Eventually it will have to. More and more companies will find themselves declaring cash returns and those companies with miniscule payouts will have to up their games. To some extent, it is that simple. Getting there will be more complicated. That is in part because competing for capital is the flip side of paying for capital. Management can just as easily be inclined to use retained earnings as contingent sources of capital to avoid having to pay investors a rich dividend. This is a modified version of the classic M&M challenge of growth. I would just note that in those expansionary postwar decades—the 1950s and 1960s—companies somehow managed to have higher yields, higher payouts, and higher growth rates. For current management teams, I would argue it is more about how capital is spent or misspent, not what they have to pay for it. Indeed, attaching a greater cash value to capital should lead to less wasteful use of it.

Dividend payout ratios for companies already paying dividends will likely rise, and large S&P 500 Index companies not currently making distributions will need to start making them. I've already referenced the top 300 companies on the Nasdaq as an area of likely change. I would also point to those NYSE dividend-paying companies that have gotten by in recent decades with low payouts and a low yield. What investors have tolerated in the past will be less tolerated going forward. I don't expect to see this overnight, but through the rest of this decade, look for each year to bring more companies into the "meaningful" payout and yield category.

That entails dozens of brand-name, large-cap companies that you recognize and use on a daily basis.

A few examples from a variety of sectors may help make the point. Consider package delivery and logistics giant FedEx. It has paid a dividend for 20 years but with a yield usually well below 1%. In mid-2022, it announced a dividend increase of over 50%. That plus a share pullback has put the yield close to 2.66% (as of 12/31/2022). That's getting close. Established retailers such as Walmart, with a payout ratio in the 40–50% range and an ~1.5% yield, also fall into the category of companies that will have to substantially increase their payout. And the big software companies such as Microsoft and Oracle with 1/3 payout ratios will feel pressure to increase their cash payouts. And then there are the zero-payers, Google and Amazon. There are plenty of smaller, less visible companies that will come to the same conclusion. An excellent company that I use in my day job, FactSet Research Systems, has a quite steady business and a 30% payout ratio and a woefully inadequate yield of ~1%. That will change. Look up your favorite old and new economy companies and prepare to position yourself accordingly.

The assertion that successful businesses will move back toward a cash relationship with company owners is striking only because we've been in such an unusual environment for several decades. But even in the very midst of the declining rate anomaly, Peter Bernstein was troubled by the prospect of successful companies not making profit distributions. Writing in 2005, he argued that:

> For a rational investor, investments that never yield cash are extremely risky. What is the difference between a painting or an ounce of gold and the stock of a company that will never pay a dividend, will never repurchase shares, will never sell out for cash or a liquid security, and will never liquidate itself? The value of both depends entirely on what somebody else will pay for the asset. These investments have no "intrinsic" value. Yes, I know about Warren Buffett and Berkshire Hathaway (full disclosure: I have shares in Berkshire Hathaway), but I also know that stock even in Buffett's company is a "greater fool" game

unless somewhere, sometime, there are positive odds on a cash payout in some form.[1]

That's not how private businesses work, and there's no reason that
being public should somehow change the basic rules of the game.
It's great to have a market; it's great to have a daily market price; it's
great to have liquidity and the option of selling. But having that
option as the only way to realize value from an investment makes
no sense, and it certainly is not businesslike.

THE MARKET'S PAYOUT AND YIELD

At the aggregate level, forecasting the increase in the dividend
payout ratio of the market is difficult, akin to guessing. And it
depends on the time frame. The market has had a payout ratio of
two-thirds in earlier periods, when dividends mattered more. It
seems unlikely but not impossible that the S&P 500 Index would
return to that figure. It is more reasonable to forecast a return to a
50% payout ratio. In recent years, the S&P 500 Index companies
have paid around $500 billion in dividends annually, with $577
billion paid in 2022. Earnings that year were $1.55 trillion, for a
payout ratio of 37%. Moving that payout up to 50% would represent an aggregate increase of $198 billion. That figure could easily
be sourced from buybacks alone, which amounted to $965 billion
in 2022. Using the numbers from the last normal, pre-pandemic
year of 2019, the incremental dollars needed to get to a 50% payout ratio are a more modest $123 billion, out of a buyback total
of $768 billion.[2] In short, this is eminently doable, with plenty of
money still left for buybacks to boost senior executive paycheck
top lines and hedge-fund bottom lines.

Dividend yield itself is determined by both the dividends available and the market price. Forecasting the latter is an exercise
well above my pay grade. Suffice it to say here that yield will be
moving up from the low level of the past three decades. Will it
settle at 3.0%, 3.5%, or 4.0%? Yes. At the end of the day, the
DCF of any investment must add up. The current 1.5% or even

a 2% yield just doesn't, no matter what the dividend growth rate is in perpetuity. The market's yield will be influenced by a variety of external factors, ranging from prevailing interest rates, the animal spirits, and our country's political economy. In almost any scenario, however, there's a lot of catching up to do for the S&P 500 Index to get to a material yield. That process involves some combination of payout ratio change, earnings growth, and index price movement. At a minimum, the implication is that index dividends will grow faster than index earnings, and that the index price would not outstrip either. Investors should be prepared for those scenarios through which the excesses of the past three decades are ameliorated.

HARVESTED CAPITAL GAINS AND BUYBACKS

Investors who have come of age during the past 30 years will push back and say that the income mandate from equities can be easily met through harvested capital gains. With steadily rising markets and dropping interest rates, that farming operation has done quite well in recent decades and offset the need for cash dividends. The market's sharp drop in 2022, particularly among the leading lights that had led the charge, calls into question investor comfort with that strategy. Harvesting capital "losses" to fund consumption can produce the same cash needed by investors, but it doesn't have the same allure as transforming gains into income. And as I discussed in Chapter 2, harvested capital gains or losses are a far cry from a dividend payment. That is not to suggest that individuals or institutions won't continue to sell assets—gains and losses—to meet current consumption needs. It is to suggest that the pressure to have proper income from capital assets will grow and result in more companies paying larger dividends. How that plays out exactly remains to be seen, but there will be a clear benefit for successful businesses that can pay a dividend, or a more material one, to start doing so. Those that can, will. There will then be a question for those that don't. Why not? Is it a choice not to, or is it a problem? What was in recent decades considered to be an attractive feature of stocks—no or trivial dividend, lots of buybacks, and M&A—will come to be considered a bug. Warren Buffett has had license to not pay a dividend. Few others will have that luxury.

What about buybacks? They have dominated the narrative and the reality of the stock market for the past three decades. They have, for all intents and purposes, replaced dividends as the definition of a successful publicly traded business—one that engages in share buybacks. I've critiqued buybacks extensively here and elsewhere. The question becomes: what will the new decade bring to this paradigm? Not surprisingly, I expect the return of genuine risk rates to be a catalyst that leads to a scaling back of companies speculating in their own shares on a massive scale. Good riddance. Buybacks epitomized the financialization of the markets—a huge academy-blessed kabuki show that goosed market returns at the expense of the real economy. Sustained declining rates created the ideal environment for that exercise. That will now change. If your investment in a particular company is dependent on a buyback for it to "work," you may be disappointed.

DIVIDEND YIELD AS VALUATION SIGNAL

For decades up until the 1980s and 1990s, the market's yield was considered a meaningful valuation variable. When the S&P 500 was created in 1957, all but a handful of its constituent members would have had a dividend and a material one at that. The newly created index had a trailing yield at year end of 4.44% and a 53% payout ratio. That is, dividends were everywhere and investors cared about them in a way that is nearly unimaginable today. In that context, the yield of the market was an input for investment decisions. Yield as a forecasting tool or factor has been used ever since, with varying degrees of diminishing accuracy as the market moved away from dividends. And that is the real problem: the market has changed. It is not that each member of the S&P 500 Index now has a low payout ratio and a low yield, suggesting low future returns. Instead, it is now the case that fully 103 companies, including many of the names leading the market, have no dividend at all (as of 12/31/2022). Something multiplied by zero is zero. Another 66 have a yield, but it is below 1%. Their distributions are simply too small to be considered a meaningful valuation or expected returns tool. There are no shades of gray here. That is 34% of the market by security count. By market cap, this situation is similar: 19% of the market has no yield; another 17.5% has a yield, but less than 1%. That is 36.5% of the market by size currently unavailable to serve as a cash-based valuation signal.

My quant friends will object here, saying that, from a total return perspective, it is easy to compare non-dividend-paying securities with higher dividend-paying ones and come to whatever conclusion the data points to. And they would be correct from a narrowly quantitative perspective. But for those investors who believe that distributable cashflow is the *sine qua non*, fundamental factor for relative and absolute valuation and expected returns, non-dividend payers just don't count. They are not part of the investable universe. To have such a large percentage of the market out of the cashflow-signaling business naturally reduces the utility of such a measure for the market's overall valuation and future returns. Over the next decade, I expect this distorted composition of the S&P 500 Index to alter. This is not a narrow market valuation call; it is a market plumbing call. When the shift occurs, dividend yield will again serve as a useful metric for assessing the overall market valuation and prospective future returns.

DIVIDEND FORMS

Another likely change ahead concerns the dividends themselves. While U.S. investors are used to the traditional quarterly payment, increased once a year, steady-as-she-goes, there are alternatives. Investors and company management teams don't like dividend cuts. It looks bad. But as we return to more companies paying more dividends, some flexibility is warranted. Companies can guide to a meaningful payout ratio of net income or free cashflow—say 60%—and then stick to it. No exceptions. If profits are up in any given year by a certain amount, the subsequent dividend increases by that amount. If profits are down, so is the dividend. Management is giving and keeping its word. At present, companies talk about paying out a certain ratio—often a range, 40–50%—but then say that the dividend will be kept at least flat even if the payout ratio rises above the stated level during periods of business weakness. That road to hell is paved with the best of intentions. The business owner is not trying to bankrupt his or her holdings. Quite the opposite. So if a company goes through a soft patch, earnings and the dividend will decline temporarily. That is not an unmanageable situation, particularly in the context of a diversified set of 30–50 such income streams. It does, however, require company executives to adhere to the stated payout rule and investors to not bolt at the first sign of temporary distress. Then market participants are not surprised or confused.

Mixing a lower, fixed dividend with flexible special dividends is another approach, sometimes seen in Asian companies or volatile cyclical ones such as energy. It has the virtue of guaranteeing a minimum income stream which is topped off, abundantly when times are good, and less so during leaner times. This too offers a combination of income for investors and flexibility for management. The current preferred format in the U.S. market is a small base dividend and the rest in buybacks at the discretion of management. That mix sounds reasonable, but it brings with it all the ills of buybacks. While we are unlikely to see dividend per terabyte of data—a modern analog to the prior practice of dividends per mile of railroad—or the return of widespread preferred shares, some shifting in payment patterns is to be expected.

DIVIDEND RISK AND DIVIDEND CUTS

The return of dividends also entails the return of dividend risk. Risk in the stock market is usually defined in terms of share prices, not cashflows. But higher payout ratios will likely mean more dividend cuts from companies that get too far out ahead of themselves. And for many dividend practitioners, it is practically a shibboleth of the trade that dividend cuts are horrible, destructive, disastrous, etc. For the managers of dividend-focused products, distribution cuts are viewed as a failure of process and a repudiation of all those PowerPoint slides that we show to due diligence analysts and clients. I have uttered such sentiments my-self in the past. But it's worth reconsidering this knee-jerk reac-tion. From an investment perspective, the occasional dividend cut from a portfolio holding should not be too concerning. It is common in investing, as in life, to navigate a continuum of risk and reward. No risk, no reward. In the stock market, the logic ap-plies to total return risk and total return reward. The definition of risk in the stock market is a miserable one, but it is what it is, the standard deviation of total returns. In some instances, individuals will reference drawdowns in share prices, or permanent impair-ment of capital. Those are all total return-oriented definitions of risk in a market which barely has a dividend. *De facto*, they are definitions of risk based almost entirely on the movement or level of share prices.

That definition of risk, I would argue, should be altered for divi-dend investors, at least for those business investors who approach the stock market as a business and are looking for cash returns from cash investments. For them, a more appropriate approach to the risk and reward continuum is dividend risk and dividend reward. The less dividend risk you take, the less dividend reward you can expect. The reward is a high-and-rising income stream; the risk is the occasional hiccough on the way to said high-and-rising income stream. In the stock setting, a portfolio approach is used to minimize individual security price risk. Well, the same can be said for cashflows. A portfolio approach minimizes the impact of any one income stream falling short—a dividend cut—on the portfolio's overall income generation.

Let me give you an example. A dividend-focused portfolio has a 4% yield. One of the holdings, Acme Roadrunner, is a 2% posi-tion and has a 6% yield. It contributes 12 basis points (12/100 of 1%) to the portfolio's overall yield. While the company has been paying and modestly increasing its dividend for years, one year the demand for Roadrunners plummets, the company has a high payout ratio and finds it necessary to cut the dividend by 50%. That is unfortunate, but such things happen. Assuming no dividend increases from any of the other 30 holdings, the yield on the original cost of the portfolio has dropped by six basis points. So instead of a 4% yield, it now has a 3.94% yield. However undesirable, that outcome is not the end of the world in a market context that yields 1.5%. And as most equities raise their dividends over time, the practical impact on a portfolio's income stream of an occasional cut from individual holdings would be even less. So let's not overdramatize the impact of a dividend cut. They should be few and far between, of course, but dividend risk is mitigated with the basic math of diversification. Twenty or 30 or 40 well-selected income streams mixed and matched mean no one mistake will materially impact the size of the check that a portfolio throws off monthly or quarterly.

There is a second element to balancing dividend risk and dividend reward. A portfolio with a lower yield has a lower risk of dividend cuts because low-yielding companies generally have lower payout ratios. But the very important offset for that lower cut risk is the lower yield itself, and the resulting reduced net present value of the income stream. Nothing ventured, nothing gained. A portfolio with a materially higher yield has a higher risk of individual cuts, but it comes with higher cashflow. Something ventured, something gained. While having a high-yielding portfolio and no dividend cuts ever is certainly an ideal outcome from a net present value perspective, a more realistic and manageable outcome is that in an effort to maximize net present value of said income stream, the portfolio will now and again experience a dividend cut from a constituent member. That is, a portfolio that is not taking dividend risk by having a very low yield or payout ratio is, in effect, leaving cash on the table. It may sound good to say that a portfolio has never had an individual security dividend cut, or that a particular ETF consists only of companies that have raised the dividend for the past 25 years—the so-called dividend aristocrats—but if that goal is achieved because of a low payout ratio and yield, the investor is playing it safe, and not maximizing the income opportunity. There's nothing wrong with that. In fact, the total return of that type of strategy may be quite attractive, but the net present value of the portfolio's distributed cashflow has not been maximized. Even if you are not an aristocrat, just a plodding burgher, and go years and years without a disruption in the distributions from one of your investments, you might want to ask, are you super smart, or are you setting an unnecessarily low bar for your investments?

RISK AND LEVERAGE

Risk and changes in interest rates are often conflated. Of course, they have a relationship. Tens of thousands on Wall Street spend every waking moment forecasting the next move in interest rates, whether it is the Federal Funds Rate directly controlled by the Federal Reserve Bank or the other tenures of the interest rate curve, especially the 10-year rate most frequently applied to stocks. In an earlier chapter, I argued why using interest rates as a base rate for the calculation of risk in equities is not a particularly good approach. Suffice it to note here that while I make no effort to forecast the future of interest rates, I am absolutely certain that after a decade of free money, risk rates—the actual discount rates used by sober investors in their assessment of a company's value—will be moving up. The golden age of zero rates is over. Financial historian Paul Schmelzing has observed that rates have been coming down steadily for the better part of 800 years.[3] I don't dispute that long-term trend. But within it are long periods—decades—when the opposite is true.

At what level of yield the 10-year will settle remains to be seen. It almost doesn't matter. The standard approach of using so-called risk-free rates and then a mystical equity risk premium has not served investors well, particularly when the risk-free rate became ultra-low and subject to too many external factors. In my day job, we use an Internal Rate of Return (IRR)—the discount rate that equates future cashflows to the present value of an investment. There is no formulaic way to determine the "right" IRR. But higher is always better than lower. A low IRR encourages investors to buy dear; a high IRR lowers the "right" price for an asset. Prepare yourself for a minimum of high-single-digit IRRs for well-established, cashflow-generative companies and double digits and more—potentially much more—for the companies beyond. That type of math will dismay those investors who have gotten used to seeing cash-burning new economy companies do well on the stock market. Such entities will be either fewer or far less valued than they have in the past. Or both.

The math of leverage is shockingly simple. When debt is cheap, say 2%, you can borrow a great deal of it and the dollar cost to service the debt is minimal. For instance, a $100 million loan costs just $2 million in interest per year, plus the amortization of the principal. That 2% "cost of carry" makes investment in 3%- and 4%-yielding projects look attractive. In short, cheap money contributes to poor decision-making. When the same $100 million costs a corporation no less than $5 million annually to service the debt (plus the repayment of principal), the investment hurdle will be much higher and likely lead to fewer wasteful acquisitions. Over the past two decades, corporate managements extolled how disciplined they were in making acquisitions and investments. They assured investors that it was a "spread" business and that as long as their returns were higher than the cost of capital, all was well. The sharp rise in interest rates and a slowing global economy in 2022 showed how wrong that argument was. But the real difference will be on existing balance sheets. Corporate America has feasted on debt for the past two decades as rates came down. Why not? Servicing the debt got cheaper with each passing year. That process will now reverse over the next decade or so as U.S. corporations slim down to make their debt service costs more manageable. What's the right level of leverage for a stable to modestly growing business? I'll let you know in a decade or so, but it most certainly won't be the levels of debt observed over the past several decades. The math simply won't permit it.

MARGINS, CAPITAL EXPENDITURES, AND EARNINGS

One constraint on the return of dividends to the U.S. stock market equation will be rising capital expenditures and operating expenses. As shown in Figure 7.1, the S&P 500 Index companies, excluding real estate and financials, have seen an increase in operating margin over the past few decades, and a corresponding decline in capital intensity. Even taking into account the shift to a service economy, we've been skimping. The argument that the S&P 500 Index was moving permanently to less capital intensive, higher profit activities now rings hollow. Outsourcing our manufacturing to China is no longer an option. Several decades of domestic underinvestment need to be addressed, putting pressure on future margins and profits. And investors viewing the S&P 500 Index as a window into the U.S. economy are likely not prepared for the pendulum to swing back toward a more moderate balance of manufacturing and service efficacy versus the prior emphasis on financial efficiency.

This pressure to meet the simultaneous demand for increased cash returns and investment may well create an M&M choice for some companies, but a reversal to a full M&M environment circa the 1950s seems unlikely. Increasing capital expenditures by 200 basis points to 8% of sales (from the current low of 6%, as indicated in Table 2.1) would cost $255 billion (using 2022 as the base year). Bringing operating margins back to 12% (as indicated in Figure 7.1) and keeping a variety of other factors unchanged would cost $328 billion. That is, the higher capital intensity and higher operating costs can easily be met by the cashflow that in recent decades has gone to buybacks and M&A activity. There is

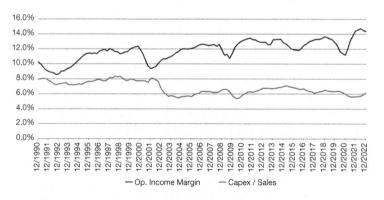

Figure 7.1 S&P 500 Index Ex. Real Estate and Financial Firms

Source: S&P Global Market Intelligence; FactSet, 2023.

still plenty of margin and cashflow to support increased invest-ment and a buttressed cash nexus of investments. While the cash is there, this investment backfilling will necessarily have an impact on near-term earnings growth.

Since 1992, index earnings have expanded at a compound annual growth rate of 7.62%—from 19.09 to 172.75—while nominal GDP has risen at a compound annual growth rate of 4.65%.[4] It's been a great ride. Keen observers will point out that U.S. companies have benefitted from higher growth rates outside the United States—think Coca-Cola—and productivity enhancers—think Google—to explain the duration and size of the gap. And they are partially correct, as are those who say that the next generation of efficiency enhancement, such as AI, will boost future earnings in the manner that Microsoft has driven office productivity since the 1990s. More generally, the S&P 500 Index is the best of the best, with a natural mechanism for slower growing or declining companies to drop out, and expanding younger companies to join the index. Thus, it has a natural edge against aggregate GDP. Perhaps, but there is a limit as to how wide the gap can be and how long it can continue.

***

All of these prospective developments will change the invest-ment framework that dividend investors have used for the past few decades. In important ways, it will make dividend investing harder than it has been. The expected increase in the opportunity set will require the discerning investor to engage more industries, particularly more cyclical, discretionary companies, and maturing information technology enterprises. That means more choices and more analyses. Whereas the dividend investor previously operated within a default investment framework, the return of cash to the U.S. stock market will expand the opportunities, and the pitfalls, of being a dividend investor in the stock market.

NOTES

[1] Peter L. Bernstein, "Dividends and the Frozen Orange Juice Syndrome," *Financial Analysts Journal*, Vol. 61, no. 2 (March–April 2005), 27.
[2] Data from Compustat of S&P Global Market Intelligence and Factset, 2023.

3 Paul Schmelzing, Staff Working Paper No. 845 "Eight Centuries of Global Real Interest Rates, R-G, and the 'Suprasecular' Decline, 1311–2018," *Bank of England Staff Working Paper no. 845* (January 2020), www.bankofengland.co.uk/working-paper/2020/eight-centuries-of-global-real-interest-rates-r-g-and-the-suprasecular-decline-1311-2018.

4 www.spglobal.com/spdji/en/indices/equity/sp-500/#overview, additional info, index earnings tab. And https://fred.stlouisfed.org/series/GDP#o adjusted for annual frequency.

8

A NEW COUNTING REALITY

Beyond the practicalities discussed in the previous chapter, the new paradigm should and may well usher in reconsideration of how we track investments. Performance tracking for investment portfolios—showing absolute and relative total return to benchmarks or peers—dates from the 1960s and 1970s, as benchmarks, portfolio information technology, and style investing came to the fore. That's all fine and good, but as the cash nexus returns to investments, it behooves investors to understand how performance is defined, measured, and presented. This chapter reviews current practices and suggests a few potential behavioral and actual measurement alterations.

THE FORGOTTEN INCOME COMPONENT OF TOTAL RETURN

To judge by the financial media, one might reasonably conclude that the mantra—"buy low, sell high, repeat frequently"—captures all you need to know about keeping score. You want stocks

DOI: 10.4324/9781003292272-9

that will go up in price ... Period. It seems simple enough. Stock prices change during the course of the day, the week, the year, and the decade. Compare the starting and ending points, and you have theoretical gains or losses. The leading indices are set up the same way. They represent a weighted basket of stock prices. As the index constituents reprice, the index adjusts accordingly. Beyond the market itself, in securities law, investment policy statements, style boxes, institutional mandates, etc., the phrase "capital appreciation" has pride of place.

But it doesn't stop there. Consider stock charts. A hundred times a day, market participants look at stock charts—a visualization of share prices over time. You want to see a slope to the upper right. A price chart that is flat is, well, flat. That can't be good. It doesn't take long for the chart to take on a life of its own—with whole legions of market participants trying to divine the future shape of the chart based on the past shape. Their whole world is the price change of an asset. To summarize, we have prices, the goal of capital appreciation, and charts moving to the upper right. This all seems straightforward enough, but it isn't a complete rendering of investment measurement. In fact, for some investors, the share price focus might be quite misleading.

Perhaps the best way to place the price chart game in proper context is to compare it to how other types of assets, such as private businesses or real estate, are measured. They too have prices, though not with the daily bids and ask that stocks have. In each case, however—more importantly—the asset owner derives some direct cash benefit from the asset that is separate from the price. In the case of private businesses or real estate, the owner gets a share of the profits or the rents. Very few people buy rental real estate or pizza parlors or franchise businesses expecting only to flip them for a higher price down the road and never taking a penny from the business in the interim. Indeed, the price of commercial real estate is very closely tied to the cashflows the buyer can expect to receive from it. ("Cap rates" without cashflows to company owners are hard to calculate, to say the least.) More generally, the price of most business assets is tied to the regular cashflows received from ownership of said asset. Maybe not the U.S. stock market, but just about every other business market operates in this fashion, and for good reason.

What's important from the perspective of measuring investment returns is—first—the realization that most assets provide an income return separate from just changes in the market price. And second, the thinking about how to value those assets is oriented much more toward the income derived from that ownership than just its near-term price in the marketplace. In fact, the sale price of an asset may not matter that much in certain instances. Do the math. If the investment has been held long enough, the benefits from the cashflows associated with ongoing ownership dwarf the difference between the purchase price and the sale price many decades later. That is particularly so if you consider the cashflows in a discounted matter—the Net Present Value.

So, in effect, we have two conceptual ways of thinking about returns. One is based on changes in the market price with little regard for the intervening period. The other is based on what I consider actual utility, with somewhat less—not zero, but somewhat less—regard for the change in market price. They are not exactly opposite approaches, but in practice they are quite different from one another.

PRICE CHARTS MISLEAD INVESTORS

Let's return from private assets to the stock market, your brokerage statement, and keeping stock-market score. As most investors understand, the proper and full accounting for an investment outcome is total return, which incorporates both the cash distributions and the change in price in a given measurement period. That's the good news. The official score-keeping system tracks both forms of return. The bad news is that on a day-to-day level, we often have two different, sometimes-at-odds-with-one-another counting systems working simultaneously: price charts and mostly price-return indices with their exclusive focus on capital appreciation, on the one hand, and the more comprehensive total return measurements running in the background. The former dominate your headlines, your media, your visual image of an investment, and your thinking. The latter show up on the back pages of your brokerage account and within the computers that track all of this. There are numerous outcomes associated with having two separate forms of mental and actual investment accounting working side by side.

First, price-only stock charts understate the apparent returns when they are used to look at a stock with a meaty dividend. As you know, when a publicly traded company goes ex its dividend (trades without the right to the upcoming payment), the price at the open of the trading session will adjust down by the amount of the dividend. That's because the amount of the dividend is now a check in the mail. Let's just say a $100 stock is going ex a $2 dividend. That day, it will likely open at or near $98. Let's say that it is a quiet day on Wall Street and it closes at that price. Total return for the day is 0%—a $2 drop in the share price offset by a $2 check in the mail. But look at the chart for that period of time. It dropped by 2%; $100 became $98. "Oh my, what happened?" is what many investors just looking at the chart would say.

Now as time goes on, the share price will recover, especially as we approach the next dividend ex-date. As long as the dividend remains flat and the market's sentiment about the company is unchanged, the price chart will essentially be horizontal, suggesting no return at all. In fact, the company's total return will be its income return. It's not hard to find stock charts that look like this. Very mature companies with little to no growth can look like this for years at a time. In an extreme instance, a high-dividend-paying company with a flat price chart can have a total return over time greater than a non-dividend-paying company that has a more typical price chart moving to the upper right. That is, a company pays a 5% dividend, does not increase it, and has a 5% annual total return and a basically flat price chart over a multi-year period. The second company does not pay a dividend, but its share price increases by 4% a year. The latter will have a better-looking chart, but a lower return. If you had to choose just between the two, which would you want?

To be fair, for a dividend-free stock, the price chart does depict total return. And there is nothing wrong with that. The problem emerges when you have the two frameworks side by side. With so many investors and analysts using this form of data visualization – price-only charts—securities with dividends are shortchanged. They just don't look as good as dividend-free competitors for capital. In Figure 8.1, I have tracked two stocks over a 20-year period. Both start at $100 per share and both have the same annual return: 8%. The tech stock's return is all share price based. The old-economy dividend stock starts with a 4% yield at time of purchase and increases the dividend by 4% a year. The share price (therefore) increases by 4% per year as well. The total return is identical, but after two decades, the price charts have diverged sharply. The tech stock is trading at a price of $466. Nicely done. Pat yourself on the back. An 8% annual return compounded over 20 years equals a 366% return, which turns $100 into $466. The dividend stock is at, uggh, $219, less than half the tech rocket. A 4% annual gain in the price translates into a lesser 119% return. That may not seem like a good deal, but it is an illusion. In terms of total return, *they are identical.* In terms of stock market sentiment, for traders, and for individual investors who bring all the psychological biases that flesh is heir to, it can mean a lot.

Now, to be fair, there are total return indices, and you can construct a total return chart for an individual security, and these charts would include the payment of the dividend, but they are

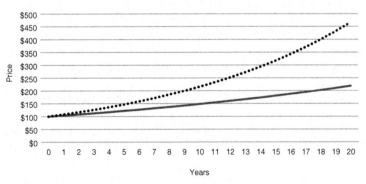

Figure 8.1 Dividend Stock versus Non-Dividend Stock Price Chart

not as popular as the price-only charts—the S&P 500 Index, the Nasdaq 100, the Russell 1000 Value, your standard stock price chart, etc. The same is true of your investment portfolio and the statements that you get. They are not always, but generally are oriented toward price changes, not total return, at least on the front pages. The back pages and the appendices will have the correct total return figures.

REINVESTMENT FALLACY

So, the charts that you see every day are not the same as the total return that you should care about. That's point one. The second point is the common counting misperception that the attractive returns of dividend-paying stocks are due only to dividend reinvestment. Wrong. This is an astonishing example of where the mental and actual accounting systems are quite out of sync with one another. The total return of an investment is fully independent of whether an investor takes the dividend as cash out of the system or reinvests it back into the stock or portfolio. Let's revisit the basics once again. Total return is the calculation in any given period—it is usually daily in the case of stocks—of the share price change and the dividend received (or gone ex-, more narrowly). That return is then geometrically linked to the next day, and to the next, and to the next. The dividend "counts" on the day it is added to the total return. And then the total return clock is reset for the next day's calculation. (The calculations can also be done weekly, monthly, or quarterly, but the returns will be slightly lower due to the less frequent compounding.)

There is a very good reason for this calculation methodology based on frequent measurement and then geometric linkage: Cash inflows or outflows of a portfolio are completely separate from the return generated by the portfolio itself. Whether the client takes out $2,000 per month or adds $5,000 per quarter has no impact on the returns generated by portfolio holdings themselves. Those inflows or outflows (including taking the dividend) just change the amount of capital available for tomorrow's total return calculation.

So while dividend reinvestment (and any other capital inflows or distributions) have no impact on the calculation of daily total return, they of course have a direct impact on the amount of money in an account. If you put more money to work, the account will be larger. If you skim off the dividends, the account will be smaller. That's just common sense. For example, if Grandma's portfolio consisted of just one dividend-paying stock generating an 8% annual return (4% dividend yield, 4% dividend growth leading to a similar amount of capital appreciation), and she reinvests the dividends, her $100 initial investment will have turned into $466 by year 20, not the $219 that she would have had had she consumed the dividends. *The total return of the investment is the same; the account values are different.*

When investment manuals talk about the power of dividend reinvestment and compounding as a miracle of wealth creation, they are correct. It is a great tool, but it is only meaningful at the account level, not at the security or portfolio total return level. There is a lot of "this makes sense once you think about it" here. The problem is that too few people stop to think about it.

IS TOTAL RETURN EVEN RIGHT?

Having pointed out these differences in counting, I want to go one step further and question whether total return itself should be the foundation of measurement in investment management. Hear me out. Maximizing total return is built deeply into the legal framework of stock market investing (SEC rules, fiduciary practices, case law, etc.), not to mention in the everyday sales and measurement of equity products. Indeed, how to maximize total return in short, intermediate, and supposedly longer-term periods is the central proposition in equity investing. My pay package, not surprisingly, has a total return component. So out of respect for the weight of that reality, I solemnly affirm that I do seek maximum total return within the framework of my specific style mandate. Let me then frame this exercise as simply asking a question about how we all do our jobs in the investment industry.

The problem is that in an environment of very low cash yields from the stock market, total return really translates into just the share price game. The problem is accentuated by the investors' short time horizons. The quest for near-term capital appreciation (daily, monthly, quarterly, annual) has become the nearly singular measure of success in the stock market. While the total return calculation naturally includes the cash payment component—the dividend—in a stock market that has consistently yielded less than 2% for decades, and has a nominal annual total return of 8–10%, that cash payment is necessarily treated as a minor player on the stage. The share price calculation can and is made daily, while dividends are generally paid only four times per year. As a result, almost all the total return math is reserved for share price changes. Managers are praised if they "outperform" the market or benchmark in any given period, and subject to disappointment if they do not.

Let me be clear that I have no opposition whatsoever to capital appreciation—to stocks going up. Most business enterprises and sensible people involved in them are keen on capital appreciation, whether that appreciation is in regard to a house, a personal business, a financial asset or a portfolio of them. I am no different. It is a matter of emphasis and focus. Keeping score is a good thing. Indeed, as I indicated earlier, until the 1960s and 1970s, there wasn't much comparison of returns versus benchmarks or peers, because the former were only just coming into existence at the time, as was the technology permitting the second. Fast forward 50 years, and we are keeping score every minute. Investor obsession with near-term relative total return has made it difficult to be a business investor in the stock market, and much easier to be a speculator. The mismatch in time frames between investor and investment is one of the great weaknesses of our current capital markets paradigm.

Measuring long-term business success with a figure that comes out daily isn't really measuring success at all. It is measuring speculation. As all good businesspeople know, successful investments usually take time. And as most attentive stock market participants know, the price of a share can change for reasons that have absolutely nothing to do with that asset. To make matters worse, stock market risk is defined in Modern Portfolio Theory (MPT) as the standard deviation and other statistical tortures of *total return*. That is, it has been focused mostly on changes in share price. At the time MPT was created, dividend return was a much greater percentage of overall total return. That is no longer the case. So the problem remains: the standard deviation of short-term changes in an asset price is *nobody's* real-world definition of risk. Yet, in a near-term total return world, it enjoys pride of place.

Some might wonder whether I am doubting the role of markets and daily liquidity more generally. Certainly not. Nor am I calling into question the long-term price discovery that markets offer. It would be almost unpatriotic in this day and age to do so. And the University of Chicago does not permit such challenges. They argue that the market price (and by derivation, anything based off of that market price) is a great virtue and perhaps the only necessary measure one needs to have. Notwithstanding the long list of Nobel Prizes from Hyde Park, Chicago's stranglehold on finance curricula, and the CFA program, I want to suggest otherwise. Near-term total return—the market's daily judgment of success and failure—need not have a monopoly on the truth. There should be a more balanced approach to measuring investment success. And high on that list of additional measures should be cash distributions made to business owners. Such distributions are the primary (albeit not the only) measure of success in the private business world. So, why not measure and track the trajectory of dividends distributed by stocks?

FOLLOW THE CASH

There are many practical reasons to broaden the measurement of performance in stock portfolios to include cash payments. While the long-term trend of the market is up, it isn't always that way. If one needs cash during a market downturn, or an individual security's retreat, the sale price can be below the purchase price, easily. That is, price returns can be negative. In contrast, a dividend payment is a dividend payment is a dividend payment. It is simple to understand and even simpler to consume. Its "return" is always positive. The money—cash on the barrel—shows up in your account. In short, it is real and tangible; share price gains are just numbers on a screen until realized with a transaction.

Yes, total return does capture the cash payment in our very low-yielding stock market, but it's worth making the extra effort to shed light on those cash distributions, their amount, and their trajectory. How would I suggest that we do that, beyond what is already indicated on many finance screens, brokerage statements, and endowment quarterly reports? As a practical matter, incorporating cash returns into portfolio measurement means counting the distributions, the current yield, the yield at cost (current income compared to the original purchase price) for an individual investment, and, most importantly, the growth rate of the income stream. You would think that would be easy? Wrong. The investment management industry is very focused on calculating and parsing total returns down to the basis point. Rest assured, there are armies of people making sure that that calculation is correct on a daily basis.

But what about the cash you actually receive from your investments? That gets somewhat less attention in part because it requires making some choices. In theory, an investment's annual yield is simple: it is the annual distribution you receive divided by the price you pay for it. In practice, it is a little trickier. Dividend payments from equities can vary, so you can either use the trailing 12-month payments or annualize the most recent quarterly payment. Both can be spot-on for an annual yield, or way off. For securities that are about to raise their dividend, or just paid a special dividend, it is a very misleading measure of yield. Nevertheless, yield is and can be tracked. That is the first step. While not considered part of performance measurement, the yield of a security or a portfolio is generally available on the internet and on third-party sites such as Morningstar or Bloomberg. Although it can be absent from the reporting of institutional accounts—I know this from experience—when I ask that the yield of an institutional account and the components of the account be included, they have been without issue. So it can be done.

TRACK THE GROWTH

The second component is the growth of the income stream. This would be a great addition to performance measurement, where it is almost entirely absent. It too can require some choices. Dividend growth is a "second derivative" function. That is, it is a consequence of something (1) that is a result of something else (2). That makes it very sensitive to small input changes. Let me give you an example. You have $1,000 invested at a 4% yield. In year one, the cash payment is $40. Next year, you are expecting a 5% increase in the dividends. Assuming you have taken the cash from the first year, in the second year you would receive a payment of $42. If it turns out to be just a 4% increase, your payment is $41.60. If it turns out to be a 6% increase, your payment is $42.40. Between a 4% and 6% increase is just $0.80. Out of capital invested of $1,000, an $0.80 difference will seem like small potatoes to most investors. But as a second derivative outcome, it matters a lot.

Similarly, the value of distributions versus the original investment—yield at cost—is highly dependent on dividend reinvestment, or other forms of capital put in or taken out. I didn't say this would be easy, just important. Then, there is the issue of special dividends, returns of capital, and other forms of distributions. Despite these challenges, however, distribution growth can and should be calculated as part of portfolio measurement. Beyond a handful of dedicated dividend managers, it rarely is. My investment team calculates growth of the dividend in our portfolios and communicates that to clients, but that reporting has no canonical status. It is extra color but does not count toward the formal measurement of performance by the industry's gatekeepers.

Why put in the time and effort to track dividend growth? Well, as indicated in Chapter 4, it is actually an excellent measure of long-term share price appreciation, of those capital gains that all investors seek. In the world of private business, the trajectory of a company's sustainable cash distributions will track its ultimate market value closely. The share price change is not the driver of the analysis—as is the case in today's low-yielding, dividend-indifferent market—but an outcome of dividend growth (underpinned by the profit growth of the business).

There is another reason to track distribution growth closely. After four decades of declining interest rates and more than a decade of low inflation, if not outright deflation, investors have become accustomed to using nominal investment returns as real (inflation-adjusted) returns. No calculations were required. Now that the inflation discount factor has returned, investors will need to keep two sets of numbers in their heads—nominal and real—for the first time in decades. Will we return to an environment where real stock market returns are the dividend yield because all dividend growth is offset by inflation? That seems unlikely, but it is a possible outcome. In any case, keeping score will necessarily become more important and involved.

WHY COUNT ANEW?

Is suggesting the use of one more measure than just the price-heavy total return so heretical? Imagine measuring the success of baseball players strictly in terms of their pay packages in the free agency market. That would be silly. Many other measures are used, and as most sports fans know, the amount paid for free agents rarely corresponds to the ultimate value realized at the team (portfolio) level. It is a strained analogy, I grant you, but the basic idea holds: Price is not always value, and change in price is not always change in value. Defenders of the current system will point out that share price changes can contain important information about future distributable cashflows. That is certainly true, and one of many reasons why share price changes, even for dividend-paying stocks, should be closely monitored. The question is one of weight and emphasis. Share prices change daily; dividends change infrequently. As a consequence, most share price changes have little to no information content about future dividends. This needs to be acknowledged.

A second objection is that tracking cash distributions does not add much to the analysis of stocks that don't pay dividends. And, I admit, despite my forecast changes in the structure of the market, those stocks still dominate for now, as they have for several decades. Performance measurement of those stocks is all about changes in the market price. There is not much more to say about them. Within a cash-based approach to portfolio construction, management, and measurement, they do not fit in. As the cash nexus increases over the next decade, however, this problem will be self-correcting. Those cashless stock market darlings will have no choice but to start paying dividends if they can afford to do so. If they cannot afford to do so, investors will understand the difference between those who can and those who can't.

How likely is a move in the direction of incorporating cash distributions into the formal measurement of stock portfolios? After three decades of strong price gains led by non- or low-dividend securities, I admit there is little chance of this notion being adopted by most investors anytime soon. But there are glimmers of hope. In addition to the communications of dividend-focused managers, I am delighted to see early signs of the return of the cash-based analysis tools to the stock market. Over the last several decades, we have conjured up a wide variety of non-cash valuation metrics out of the simple necessity that you can't count what is not there. When investors once again begin to demand cash for their capital, however, many of the textbook tools that rely on cash will find utility again. So dust off your textbooks and refamiliarize yourself with genuine DDMs, NPVs, and IRRs (my preferred metric). Cashflow to management will no longer be sufficient. It will once again be cashflow to the end investor. The shift should allow company owners to spend more time considering long-term cashflow forecasting, not near-term quarterly earnings or ephemeral price targets. One tool in particular warrants greater attention. We turn to that now.

DURATION

In the upcoming cashflow-will-once-again-mean-something environment, there is an analytical tool that engaged investors can use to assess asset types and individual investments. And that is duration. It helps investors decide between the options of a little bit of cash now with more growth later, or more cash up-front but less increase of the income stream. Spoiler alert: cash up-front is generally better. The concept of duration was created in 1938 by Canadian economist Frederick Macaulay. Macauley's original formula, known as Macaulay duration, comes up with the length of time a bond investor has to wait to receive the net present value of the cashflows from the bond or a portfolio of bonds. It is a measure of time. The higher the number, the longer it takes you to get your (discounted) money back. When you then layer in a change in interest rates used to discount those cashflows—and therefore change your payback period—you have a back-of-the-envelope tool to measure the change in the "proper" price of said bond or portfolio. The higher the duration, the greater the impact of an interest rate change on the bond price because there is more time for the discounting process to impact the present value of the cash-flows. The lower the duration, the less the window of opportunity for a change in interest rates to have on the price.

Macauley duration can also be used as a rule-of-thumb tool to compare cashflows within and across asset classes. And if we na-ively assume that stock-market investors are interested in maxi-mizing their cashflow and equally naively keep all other factors and considerations unchanged—they would prefer a portfolio with a lower duration rather than a higher one. For them, rising interest or risk rates would, in theory, do less damage to the price of the lower-duration portfolio. In the bond world, a shorter ma-turity is the easiest way to have a lower duration. In a declining rate environment, in contrast, longer duration investments will benefit more in terms of capital appreciation. That latter condi-tion has, broadly speaking, been the operating environment for the three decades prior to 2022.

Although typical stock investors have not cared a whit about cashflows over the past three decades as they searched for the next unicorn, duration analysis will be a useful tool as cash makes a comeback. When I first argued a decade ago for investors to use duration, cash rates of return were still low and declining. The idea garnered little traction. Now they are not zero, and it is worth revisiting duration as applied to the stock market. But it won't be easy. In a traditional fixed-income duration calculation, most of the variables are set—you know the current price of the bond, the amount of the coupons and the principal, and the current interest rate. Change the interest rate and calculate. For equities, the math is a lot harder. Equity coupons—the dividends—generally grow over time, so you need to calculate that into the equation. And then there is the matter of the terminal value. With simple bonds, you have a date of maturity when your principal is returned. That principal value gets discounted back to the present time. For eq-uities, there is no date of maturity. So either you calculate the duration of the income stream out in perpetuity, which is tricky, or you come up with a terminal value of the stock some time out, and discount it back to the present time, which is trickier. Finally, there is the matter of the right discount rate to use.

While duration is not a common way of viewing equities or a precise way of valuing them, it remains useful at the broadest level. Even without doing all the math, one consequence stands out. A stock portfolio offering current material cashflows (dividends) will necessarily have a lower duration than one with no or low current cashflows. That's for the simple reason that there are up-front payments which get reduced less by an increase in interest or risk rates. Think about that when you consider the standard notion that growth stocks will do better in a rising rate environment because they will keep up with inflation better. Maybe yes, maybe no, but without an income stream (or just a minimal one) that rises along with the rates, the math of duration suggests otherwise.

On my website, I have presented the math of duration under three simple scenarios.[1] The first is the U.S. stock market as represented by the S&P 500 Index with its paltry 1.5% cash yield, but higher dividend growth rate. Its duration under a variety of growth scenarios is in the 70-year range. That's long and highly subject to the vicissitudes of rate changes. On the other hand, a portfolio with a yield of 4.5% but lower dividend growth has a duration of about 24 years. The so-called dividend growth market, which occupies a lot of retail shelf space, has a duration of around 36 years when the yield is 3% and dividend growth between the other two. So that's the range of weighted payback periods as rates move around. Remember, this is not a tool to forecast share price changes. It is just the payback period. The price sensitivity is a matter for the stock market to decide. But you can be sure higher rates will take their pound of flesh out of all those cashless darlings that have been dominating the news for the past decade.

If duration is a bit too complex, there are simpler ways to understand the benefits of getting paid up-front in a nonzero, real risk-rate environment. In the *Strategic Dividend Investor* (from 2011), I compare the income stream from a portfolio yielding 5% and growing the dividend at a rate of 5% annually to an income stream yielding 2% and growing the distribution 8% per year. Both portfolios have the same expected annual return of 10%. But despite the higher growth of the 2 + 8 portfolio, it takes a whopping 33 years for the annual income of that portfolio to equal the annual payments from the 5 + 5 portfolio. This is not a duration calculation, but just a common-sense glimpse at cashflow management. And it should not come as a surprise that a rise in the discount rate will have a far greater impact on the "growth" portfolio than on the one offering the higher current cash distribution.

Defenders of the low or no-cashflow approach are put in a tricky position if they want to pay nominal obeisance to the discounted cashflow framework that still underpins most valuation exercises on Wall Street, even for non-dividend-paying stocks. Their only real answer is that once their distributable cashflow-free companies have grown to a certain scale and profitability, they will begin to make distributions of such size and growth rates as to justify the many upfront years of no or low payments. In *Getting Back to Business* from 2018, I used the example of a leading online retailer whose cash distributions may start in a year, in a decade, or never. In 2022, that retailer reported revenue of an astounding $514 billion. After accounting for the cost of goods sold, it had gross profits of $235 billion. Still, the company reported a net loss of $2.7 billion, and free cashflow after capital expenditures was negative $17 billion. Perhaps one day it will be big enough – "have enough scale"—to be able to afford to pay a dividend. Just not today. The math of duration, however, is unequivocal: Those long-deferred payments, no matter how much is expected or forecasted by stock promoters, will be worth a lot less today if risk rates remain above the near-zero level.

THE INVESTMENT MATH OF DOWN MARKETS

The return of the cash nexus should affect how investors think about market math in another, important manner. The U.S. stock market declined by nearly 20% in 2022. No one was particularly happy about that, but the rapid reset of prices does provide an opportunity to remind investors about basic investing math. In this case, the issue is expected future returns after a sharp move in the market, either up or down. And that math is somewhat paradoxical. Consider, for instance, investment in the income stream—the dividends—of a diversified portfolio of stable, publicly traded companies. The cash yield at time of purchase in 2021 for $100 is 4%, or $4. Fast forward to December 31, 2022, and the price of the portfolio has declined by a quarter to $75. The new cash yield for reinvested dividends or new money in the portfolio has become 5.33%. That is, the expected annual cash return has increased by a third. That assumes all other things being kept equal, including no dividend growth or cuts in the interim or in the immediate future. In this particular instance, with the economy slowing, even typical, non-cyclical, dividend payers will eventually be affected. Dividend growth may slow. Some companies may even cut their distributions. But in a diversified portfolio context, the likelihood of a material reduction in the portfolio's overall distribution is small. So, as a practical matter, a decline in the market price of a portfolio income stream necessarily leads to an increase in the expected future cash return of said income stream.

That math runs counter to the stance of typical investors who shudder at the thought of any share price decline. It runs counter to Wall Street's scoring system that focuses on asset prices—measured daily—not asset utility. It runs counter to a fee system based on asset values—the amount you pay your broker is based on the value in your account, not the income generated by it. Of course, it is true that even for investors focused on income streams, the share price very much matters at the time of purchase (when low is much better) and at the time of sale (when high is much better). But in between those two points—whether it is five months, five years, or five decades—share prices matter a good deal less than the amount and direction of the income stream. And temporarily lower share prices in the intermediary period actually allow for higher future returns for the reinvestment of dividends from a given income stream. This logic has its limits. As long as the income stream increases or at least does not decline materially, there is a floor to the share price. Otherwise, the yield gets too high and opportunistic investors rush in.

Let me be clear: I'm not rooting for down markets, but the math is the math. So back to 2022. If you happened to own a diversified portfolio of material income-producing equities coming into the year, your NAV was certainly hit hard. And given the widely held view at the time that the economy was slowing down, one would reasonably expect a portfolio's dividend growth to slow temporarily. Still, reinvested dividends from the portfolio or new money would be buying essentially the same income stream but at a lower cost. For most investors, that's a good deal. Now let's compare this dynamic to what happens when stocks without income streams suffer a sharp decline. Does the expected future return increase? Perhaps. I don't know. There's no cash return to calibrate your expected future return. You can always hope for the recovery of the P/E multiple to get the stock price back up, but that requires the agreement of thousands of people and computers buying the share back up to the prior P/E multiple. That may or may not happen, and it's a very different investment case compared to one anchored around a income stream.

***

The logic of cash measurement or discounting is neither popular nor unpopular. It just is. Cash is cash. And business investors with a cash sensibility and the ability to see through near-term share price moves can use underutilized cash-based tracking systems to measure and manage their portfolios. Obviously, holders of non-cashflow securities and near-term traders care not a whit about these calculations, at least for now. We will see if that continues if real risk reenters the investment equation more than a decade after it was abolished by central banking authorities.

NOTE

[1] https://strategicdividendinvestor.com/equity-duration-revisited-for-an-even-lower-market-yield/.

9

THE POLITICAL ECONOMY OF SUSTAINABILITY

The global neoliberal order of recent decades featured finance less constrained by prior social, political, and regulatory concerns. Capital moved freely; capital triumphed. This chapter briefly reviews how that paradigm came about, and then shifts to how it came undone. It offers a preliminary outline of what a new political economy might be like. Of particular interest is how the current clarion call for sustainable investing fits into the upcoming paradigm's emphasis on a cash nexus.

THE IMPORTANCE OF POLITICAL ECONOMY

Investors underestimate the importance of political economy. Our financial institutions rely on our political structures, and our political framework really works only because of certain underlying economic relationships. Separating the two realms is impossible. Think about how critical the rule of law, the inviolability of contracts, individual liberty, and an independent judiciary are for the functioning of capital markets. And in the other direction, private

DOI: 10.4324/9781003292272-10

property, commerce, and entrepreneurship create the foundations for the liberal political order.

Adam Smith might be considered the first modern political economist. Karl Marx wrote about political economy in a highly argumentative fashion, but in terms of appreciating the interdependence of the two spheres, he was perfectly lucid. Friedrich Hayek and Milton Friedman, among many others, continued to intertwine politics and economics in their analysis. In recent decades, Francis Fukuyama has been identified broadly with the market-friendly political economy paradigm which dominated until just a few years ago. The point here is not to review three centuries of political economy, but to remind investors who don't often think of the broader context of investing that *political economy is the broader context* and that it matters a lot. Finance professionals and politicians tend to stay in their respective lanes and thus poorly understand how the overall highway system works. Moreover, most individuals within a political economy mode naturally assume it will continue in perpetuity. While modes can last for many years, decades, or even centuries, they do change. We are experiencing one of those changes right now.

THE END OF THE GLOBAL NEOLIBERAL ORDER

Why should political economy matter to market participants? Because we are exiting a period that has been labeled—for better or worse—the "global neoliberal order" or the epoch of "neoliberalism." While there is no canonical definition of neoliberalism, and the term itself has a long and somewhat convoluted history, there is some consensus that it became dominant in the 1980s and has been characterized by the globalization of trade, labor, and markets. Neoliberalism has benefitted from widespread deregulation of financial activity and the privileging of market relationships in determining economic outcomes. The paradigm was bolstered by a generally benign geo-political environment—the Soviet Union had gone away, China had not yet arrived as a political superpower, and U.S. hegemony was clear. Within the United States, there was a broad consensus among politicians and business leaders that all of these developments were in our collective interest. While the decline in interest rates starting in the 1980s in the United States is not usually considered an explicit component of neoliberalism's advance, falling risk-free rates clearly lubricated the mechanical parts of the neoliberal engine.

So what did neoliberalism bring to the art and practice of stock market investing in the United States? Very high returns. That might sound good, but critics of the development have labeled it the "financialization" of investment. That structural goosing of returns violated Miller & Modigliani's still-wise 1958 invocation that the enterprise value of an investment should depend on the underlying productivity of the assets, not how they are packaged. *Financialization brought a lot of fancy packaging.* Declining interest rates and the securities law change in 1982 opening the floodgates to buybacks created a straightforward path for company executives to boost nominal equity returns via leverage. As investors shifted their gaze from cash dividends to screen share prices, every effort was made to push up the latter. Compensation based on share prices rather than actual dividends paid ensured that executives were incentivized to focus on the stock, not the underlying cashflows. New valuation markers such as EBITDA and Adjusted EPS further attenuated the role of cash in the valuation exercise. Thomas Piketty loudly objected in 2014 that returns on capital had become higher than underlying economic growth.[1] At least in the case of the U.S. stock market, the *léger de main* had worked. As Julius Krein has pointed out, this widening gap between returns and actual growth had profound implications for the reigning model of political economy:

> A more comprehensive explanation would simply state that the U.S. economy is, to a unique extent, organized around maximizing asset values and returns on capital independently of growth. ... This may seem obvious or even tautological: what is capitalism if not a system aimed at maximizing returns on capital? But the disconnect that has emerged between returns on U.S. financial assets and underlying economic performance—and even corporate profits—over the last few decades should raise deeper questions about basic economic policy assumptions and their theoretical foundations.[2]

We have just begun the process of rethinking this political economy framework. In the meantime, it is fair to note that speculation within the neoliberal market model worked well for many, but especially for stock-market investors. On the other side of the ledger, larger than normal wealth gaps, the gutting of the U.S. middle class and a stunning deindustrialization of the U.S. economy resulted. And those trends are most certainly not sustainable.

Then came Donald Trump, China and COVID, and Russia invading Ukraine. They did not cause the end of the global neoliberal order, but they reflected its demise. Visibly from 2016 onward, the consensus in the U.S. evaporated, not only about particular economic or political models but even about the need to have a consensus at all. A few years later, almost overnight, having tight global supply chains and outsourcing our manufacturing to China no longer seemed like a great idea. And most recently, Russia's invasion of Ukraine has shattered the notion of the liberal ideal prevailing globally. The return of nonzero interest rates (and therefore genuine investment risk), most evident in 2022, seized up the formerly well-lubricated neoliberal capital markets.

TRUST AND THE NEW ORDER?

So where are we heading? It is too early to say for sure, but it is clear enough that the pendulum is now swinging back from the finance industry's easy advances of the past several decades. Milton Friedman's shareholder capitalism is being challenged by a broader European stakeholder approach taking into account factors beyond just financial returns. The economic model of extreme globalization will have to be altered, with a greater emphasis on onshoring, friendshoring, and nearshoring. Expect to see more regional and national, and less global. Expect more regulation rather than less regulation. One of the few points of agreement between both major U.S. political parties is their axe to grind against the tech companies that led the neoliberal stock market for decades.

Many other elements of the incoming political economy remain to be determined. Of those elements, politics in the U.S. may end up being the most important for investors. The utter lack of trust in our political institutions (circa 2023) runs the risk of bleeding over into the investment realm. What's the difference between, say, Venezuela and Argentina, on the one hand, and Switzerland, on the other? The former have vibrant populations, natural resources, and desirable geographies. The latter has … beautiful mountains and a history of fine watchmaking. Yet assets in the former countries trade at single-digit "multiples," if that, while assets associated with Switzerland trade at sky-high premiums, and have for decades. Why? Because of the trust in the institutions and practices underpinning those assets. U.S. assets trade with a trust factor properly closer to that of Switzerland. The United States benefits from its status as global hegemon, reserve currency provider, and all the other advantages of incumbency. But given the current precarious state of governance in the United States, that trust and those benefits are very much at risk. In short, our political economy matters, far more than most investors appreciate.

The level of trust in our new political economy will play out over years if not decades. In the meantime, from a narrower U.S. stock market perspective, more specific outcomes associated with the end of the neoliberal order are likely. The first is consistent with the end of interest rates declining, the dominant theme of this work. The resulting return of material risk rates will leave less room for "excessive trust" tricks of the trade that became so common during the final decade of the prior order. SPACs, unicorns, and accounting shenanigans to optimize EPS should become scarcer. And then there is return of the cash nexus. The new political economy will provide another reason for it: a different level of trust. The post-neoliberal order will likely entail less trust in corporate executives and greater insistence by investors on a tangible return for their capital.

TRUST AND THE U.S. DOLLAR

There is ample evidence that the U.S. dollar is moving to the right on the trust–distrust spectrum. China and selected other foreign powers would love to see the United States lose its reserve currency status, though there is no clear path for that to occur in the near-term. Still, many investors assume it is time for a new currency, one notably independent of trust-unworthy state actors such as central bankers and government treasury or tax officials empowered by new technology to control access to currency, down to the individual consumer. While supporters of alternative currencies believe they have plenty of reason to distrust the surveillance state, it is not clear to me that an alternative currency gets around the challenge of trust. Much of the current backlash against globalism is a rejection of the large, unelected, transnational organizations that have prospered over the past few decades. The initial move appears to be back toward smaller, more local entities. While a currency based on decentralized computer networks might not be in the hands of existing state actors, it is in the hands of the software developers and those who operate the networks. You can't escape trust. As the early innings of DeFi (decentralized finance) show, the challenges aren't about distributed ledgers or encryption or new stores of value. They are about human folly. A digital store of value just transfers the trust equation from parties you know to parties you don't know. There is much more to come on this topic.

That being said, I would not be entirely surprised to see a new currency emerge along with the new political economy. That is because while distributed ledgers are not new, the internet is well suited to implement distributed ledger technology that is faster and more expansive than could ever have been previously imagined. And a digital economy would benefit from a native system of measurement, store of value, and medium of exchange. Prior and existing currencies such as blocks of salt, strings of beads, gold coins, paper backed by gold coins, paper not backed by gold coins, and ledger entries of said prior currencies—much of our current system—may not be as fit-to-purpose. They have a lot of baggage and are not native to a digital environment. Still, coming up with a widely accepted medium of exchange will involve numerous iterations, including the obligatory long list of failed ventures and fraudsters taking advantage of a new environment. The use case, logic, and base value (as in store of value) will have to be far clearer than it has been heretofore if an alternative currency is to gain traction with a broader community.

CAPITAL, LABOR, AND STOCK-BASED COMPENSATION

While the precise nature of the new political economy has yet to emerge, it is already clear that the Capital–Labor relationship will need to be refreshed. There was a time and place when political economy was all about the relationship between the two. That is no longer even remotely the case. Three full decades of globalization and deregulation have meant that any presumed balance has been discarded in favor of the employers. Recent union contract renewals suggest some moderation or even reversal in that trend. In the broader political economy realignment to come, however, there is another area where an existing capital markets practice might be part of the new paradigm.

That practice is stock-based compensation (SBC). In its current variant, SBC is a largely cashless exercise. Among start-up and pre-revenue and pre-profit companies, it is used to hire and retain employees. Management pays in shares because it has no cash to do so. With the prospect of a cashout down the road via an IPO or an acquisition, SBC is that pot of gold at the end of the stock market rainbow. For larger, more successful companies, especially those in the new economy, SBC is a form of enhanced compensation for employees. Large grants of options or restricted stock are supposed to align the interests of executives and shareholders. Because these companies often have no or *de minimis* dividends—think the FAANGS et al.—the focus is necessarily on the share price. As a result, this compensation tool shares the same flaw of harvesting capital gains versus getting a dividend: The only way to realize any value at all is by selling the shares in the casino. Share ownership is not encouraged; share selling is.

More relevant here is that the current form of SBC offers a visible manifestation of the state of relations between management and employees. In Silicon Valley, nobody may see the problem. It has been a path to riches for those in the tech economy. In the broader economy, however, SBC of dividend-free and dividend-light stocks is a pitch-perfect example of the hollow "financialization" of the capital markets. In this context, rank-and-file employees of mature companies, if they get shares at all as part of their compensation, have little incentive to keep them. They have plenty of reasons to be suspicious. Older employees might recall Enron, where a retirement plan loaded with company shares—around 60% of total plan assets—devastated the retirement plans of employees when the company collapsed in just a few months in 2001. Company shares are still eligible to be included in company-sponsored 401(k) programs but are viewed with a well-warranted degree of suspicion. Employees with the option of owning company shares are warned about the risk of "doubling down" on company risk—their day jobs and their retirement accounts. The fiduciary responsibility of program administrators contributes to the caution about too heavy a concentration in company shares.

With that history and those restrictions in place, suggesting that employees of publicly traded companies should once again have access to company shares needs a strong justification. That justification is the return of the cash nexus. Here, it might be helpful to look at past practice. The creator of the initial Employee Stock Ownership Plan (ESOP) in 1956, the attorney and political economist Louis Kelso, saw employee ownership of companies as a boon for many reasons. The challenge was in financing the purchase of the shares since few employees could afford them outright or borrow money to do so. (These shares were not being granted by the company; they were being purchased from the original company owners.) His innovation was in having the company's retirement plan, as a separate legal entity, borrow the money to purchase company shares, and *use the dividends—yes the dividends—to help pay back the loan.* The idea made sense only because successful companies paid dividends at the time. As the Louis Kelso Foundation website states, he created "the prototype of the leveraged buy-out ... to enable working people without savings to buy stock in their employer company and pay for it out of its future dividend yield."[3] Kelso's original version of the ESOP was unwieldy, narrow, and designed mostly as a succession tool. It became less unwieldy as a result of the 1974 Employee Retirement Income Security Retirement Act (ERISA). Employee ownership of shares became easier still with the introduction of the 401(k) program in 1978.

With the upcoming change in our political economy, it is time to revisit employee ownership. I tried to do so a decade ago in *The Dividend Imperative* (2013). At the time, the idea got no traction. Rates were still going down, and non-dividend-paying stocks were still going up. But fast forward a decade and yield matters again. In that context, employee ownership of shares in large successful, cash-generative companies with material dividends now makes sense. The format—ESOP, 401(k), taxable accounts—matters less than the incentive. Employees getting a material and rising dividend have a reason to hold the shares, watch the checks come in, and be aligned with other shareholders and management. A major French company, TotalEnergies, is already there. Its press release from early 2023 authorizing additional shares for employees is a great description of the idea, with the company noting the 700 million euros in dividends received by employees during the previous year.[4] With a yield of around 5% per year in cash dividends, the TotalEnergies shares are desirable to hold, not sell, upon vesting.

As dividend yields rise for the U.S. market, I expect many large cashflow-generative companies with currently no or low dividends to move in this direction. Having employees get access to the dividend-paying shares of their enterprises will not remedy decades of narrower, more speculative SBC, nor will it magically erase centuries of enmity between Capital and Labor. As a minor but highly symbolic part of employee compensation, however, SBC might constitute an effective nudge leading to some greater alignment of effort between the various parties in the new political economy.

SUSTAINABLE INVESTING

While the tug-of-war between Capital and Labor hearkens back to prior periods, the current emphasis on sustainable investing is new, or at least appears to be. For the cash-focused investor, however, sustainable investing may be more the evolution of an existing practice rather than an entirely new one. Between the time this was written and the time when you read it, the definitions, debates, and data around sustainable investing will have changed, so I will limit my comments to high-level observations from a cashflow-based perspective. And in that regard, the assertion is straightforward: dividend-focused investing was "sustainable" decades ahead of the current frisson. That's no statement of bravado or claim of originality. Think about it. The attraction of an income stream—whether of a publicly traded or closely held asset—is its value over time. Whereas a "price-only" asset can be bought tomorrow with the intention of selling it a week or month from now, an income stream-based asset delivers its worth over many years.

Investors might agree or disagree as to the current value of an income stream—and put a changing, daily price on it—but the NPV of the income stream is measured in decades. If the cashflow is not sustained, or is deemed unsustainable, the math falls apart immediately. Investors and company management might be right or wrong about what they believe to be sustainable—natural gas-fired electricity generation versus nuclear versus wind and solar, EVs versus ICEs, plastic bottles replacing glass, etc.—but very few if any executives are explicitly thinking only about today and tomorrow. All are trying to create enterprises that endure for decades. Even something as ephemeral as the fast fashion business model has to be sustainable in some sense if it is to have more than just a few iterations.

The sustainability model applies even to young, cashflow-free companies, at least those that wish to be taken seriously. Their main goal—think biotechs, media start-ups, and consumer companies – is to get purchased by a larger enterprise. Their timeline may be near-term—the next few years—but the purchaser laying out the cash still has to be doing the math of long-term cashflow sustainability. Does the purchased asset assist in that company's own long-term planning? Even if an enterprise is to change hands several times, the ultimate buyer has no choice but to do the long-term cashflow calculations. In this regard, all serious ventures fall into a framework of intended (if not always realized) sustainability.

So dividend-focused investors are expecting their real estate, private enterprises, and even publicly traded companies to be operating for decades. That means we also expect the businesses to evolve along with their customers and society in general. For instance, a forecast for The Coca-Cola Company a little more than a hundred years ago when the shares began trading on the NYSE might not have had original fountain Coca-Cola mostly replaced by bottled or canned Coke, but over time that happened. More recently, the original sugar version was supplemented by Diet Coke which has been further revised by Coke Zero. Did the investor in the KO share a century ago know what the company would be selling now? Of course not, but they knew that management was trying to move along with society's demand for and definition of desirable beverages. They have to. Major manufacturing facilities can take years to build and are expected to last decades. If the company spends hundreds of millions on the Fresca-flavored popsicle line, they have to have a reasonable belief that Frescapops (made up) will be around for a long time, or that the line can be repurposed to follow consumer tastes. They may be right or wrong in that judgment, but all non-speculative capital asset deployment is, by definition, long term in nature. Stranded assets are a risk, of course, but that comes with the territory in any business.

Current definitions of sustainability go well beyond the simple matter of consumer preferences. There are urgent global problems that sustainable investing is trying to help solve or at least not worsen. Indeed, the goalposts have moved a lot in recent years with the rise of Environmental, Social & Governance (ESG) investing as the formal framework for assessing and promoting sustainability. In this regard, Coke is facing new challenges regarding its packaging, water usage, product content, and carbon generation. These incremental concerns make investing in or managing companies all the harder, but they do not change the timeline or intention of having a sustainable business model. While I can't be certain that The Coca-Cola Company will be around 50 years from now paying robust dividends, I do know that KO's management is well aware of not only evolving consumer preferences but also the evolving nature of its "societal license to operate"—the legal, political, and cultural environment that allows large corporations to function and flourish. Being a minority shareholder means acknowledging the agency cost of having the Coke board and management determine their appropriate sustainability strategy in regard to sustainability.

Corporate managements "getting it right" is only half the challenge. The still-young ESG investing framework has had more than a few false starts and what might be considered unexpected outcomes. For instance, Germany's Greens have engaged in a half-century struggle against nuclear power. At the very moment of their victory in 2023—the shutting down of the country's remaining nuclear plants—their stance appears extraordinarily dangerous for both Germany and the environment. To put it in finance theory terms, the ESG policy marketplace is still highly inefficient from an information and outcome perspective. That inefficiency creates great challenges and opportunities for investors and companies alike. For instance, a small portion of the ESG community features a knee-jerk reaction calling for much higher corporate investments and much lower distributions. While that is certainly one option—akin to putting the economy on a war footing—there have been previous bouts of seemingly unlimited capital allocation that looked more like bubbles than sustainable investment.

I believe that the upcoming return of the cash nexus and genuine risk rates will lead to more *discriminating* investment in environmental, social, and governance mitigation, not just more investment. In the end, there will be less waste of (what had previously been nearly free) capital. If so, that will be good for investors, for society, and for the planet. Despite having to operate within the new ESG framework for assessing sustainability, investors and managers will find some things do not change: few enterprises paying dividends to shareholders consciously and intentionally allow business to dry up without trying to sustain it. There are certain exceptions, such as self-liquidating enterprises, where it is not realistic to have decades-long cashflow forecasts. But such exceptions rarely dominate serious dividend-focused portfolios. Intention may be one thing; execution is another. When either company management or investors make a mistake—such as Kodak or Avon during their respective declines—having a diversified portfolio minimizes the impact on the portfolio's income stream of having an individual company fail in its own effort to sustain itself for the next half-century.

***

The dominant form of political economy in the Western world is changing. There is no doubt that we are moving away from the global neoliberal model of the past several decades. The bigger question is how far away we will move from the broader capitalist, market model of the past several centuries. I'll leave the answer to the futurists, but there are two practical implications of this shift. First, it is fair to assume that the legal and regulatory frameworks will be slower to evolve and will have to catch up with whatever new model replaces the current order. There are risks to being a late adopter; there are also risks to being in the vanguard. Once again, investors (and company managers) will face the challenge of decision-making under conditions of uncertainty. That is a constant, regardless of the political economy model. Second, a shift in political economy does not change the rules of math. Discounted cashflows, net present values, etc. are not subject to evolving societal preferences. The inputs might be affected, but the basic analytical framework cannot be. If the math itself becomes politicized—if your children are taught at school that 2+2 does not equal 4 because it is an artifact of an oppressive culture—you can safely disregard everything in this book.

NOTES

[1] Thomas Piketty, *Capital in the Twenty-First Century* (Cambridge, MA: Cambridge University Press, 2014).

[2] Julius Krein, "The Value of Nothing: Capital vs. Growth," *American Affairs*, Vol. 5, no. 3 (Fall 2021), https://americanaffairsjournal.org/2021/08/the-value-of-nothing-capital-versus-growth/.

[3] The Kelso Institute, https://kelsoinstitute.org/louiskelso/kelso-paradigm/who-what-and-why/ (accessed November 13, 2023).

[4] TotalEnergies website, https://totalenergies.com/media/news/press-releases/totalenergies-number-2-employee-share-ownership-europe-launches-its (accessed November 13, 2023).

10

WHAT TO LOOK FOR IN THE NEXT DECADE

How can investors position their portfolios for this new paradigm? To some extent, the task has already gotten easier. The rise in interest rates in the early 2020s means that fixed-income and cash-like instruments now have material yields. Their investors get to pick and choose yields, maturities, risk, and duration profiles in a way that they have been unable to do for much of the previous decade. The question remains equities. The stock market has not yet adjusted to the coming environment, and the reversion to the cash nexus there may take years. In the meantime, this chapter offers just a few examples of what I consider will be important factors to consider in the upcoming paradigm. These are certainly not rigid criteria for investment, but they are topics I will be pursuing in the years ahead.

FOLLOW THE CASH

Chapter 4 outlined how to be a dividend investor in a dividend-light stock market. Many of those approaches will become even

DOI: 10.4324/9781003292272-11

more important in the years to come as the overall market shifts its focus. The good news is that all the necessary tools are hiding in plain sight. They are the largely ignored but the still-in-place cashflow-based metrics of valuation and investment: the DDMs, DCFs, NPVs, and IRRs. The key will be to apply those tools seriously to the increased number of companies that will be competing for investor attention on the basis of distributable cashflows. I earlier discussed possible candidates (not least among the major tech companies), but beyond those cited, there is also an opportunity to identify those companies likely to meet investors halfway in the years ahead.

To do so, the engaged investor can follow the cash backward and determine which companies are in the best position to become material dividend payers. Start with pricing power. In the period of disinflation if not actual deflation over the past decade (and broadly the past several), pricing power mattered, but not as much as it might have. Getting the right balance between volume and price is tricky for any business in any environment, but in a deflationary period, the market's thumb was pressing the scale in favor of volume. Take market share; worry about profitability later. For emerging businesses, that will always be a consideration. But in the years ahead, where inflation may well be a genuinely positive number, the ability to have at least some degree of control over price—whether through brand strength, distribution heft, or product innovation—will matter even more. I'm not making a call in favor of inflation. Instead, this is a call on how to manage in an environment when disinflation is less prominent. Productivity gains due to technological advances—AI is all the rage as I finish this book—will continue to put pressure on pricing, as they have for many decades. But productivity gains in a deflationary environment will look different from those in a non-deflationary environment. In short, pricing power matters. Companies that have it will find themselves in a better condition to generate distributable cash.

Access to cash will also matter because companies will need extra flexibility to fund operations. I earlier highlighted my expectation of some mean reversion in the operating margins (approximately

200 basis points) of the S&P 500 Index companies, as companies spend to make up for years of underinvestment associated with the prior paradigm built around outsourcing. Those companies that have either pricing power, structurally attractive margins, or some combination of both will be in a better position to build more durable and more vertically integrated supply and distribution models. Those value chains will cost more, but they will also be worth more over time, because the companies will be better able to withstand operating in a less benign political and regulatory environment.

While we are still on the income statement, look for fewer accounting shenanigans. Call me naively optimistic, but declining interest rates and a tolerant financial media provided cover for a multitude of managerial sins that made adjusted earnings and special measures of operations and valuation all too common and accepted. The stock market outliers that benefitted from the flattering "financialization" packaging of the prior order will have to do without now that real risk rates have returned. While some publicly traded companies will continue to abuse investors and test the limits of regulatory authorities, there might just be less of it. While it is not impossible to fake levels of cash being generated by a business—Enron perfected the art—it is harder than the now widely accepted accounting abuse done to earnings. Comparing the cashflow statement (only introduced in 1988) with the income statement is a good start. Large and sustained difference between net income and free cashflow, especially in mature companies, is a clear warning sign.

FOCUS ON THE BALANCE SHEET

As notable as changes on the income statement will be, those on the balance will be even more important. Indeed, the decades of declining interest rates allowed managers and investors to largely ignore balance sheets. If the past decade was about the anything-goes income statement, this one will be all about shoring up company finances and resources. That's where I will be engaging corporate management in the years ahead. This shift in priority will manifest in any number of ways. The most obvious one will be leverage—the ratio of borrowed money (debt) to the investors' own capital (equity) in an enterprise. Using much more debt worked in favor of companies and investors in the decades when interest rates declined. If rates no longer decline, that tailwind will be removed. If rates rise, leverage will necessarily have to be reined in. Where a net debt to EBITDA (earnings before interest, taxes, depreciation, and amortization) ratio of five might have been acceptable with rates falling, the new normal might be three.

Over the past few decades, companies became all too comfortable telling investors that their BBB and BBB– ratings (the lowest investment grade) indicated that they had "fortress" balance sheets. I heard that countless times during meetings with management and on quarterly conference calls. Fortunately, the rise in rates since 2021 has very quickly dispatched those statements of bravado. Less leverage may entail slower rates of growth, but it should—all other factors being held equal—also produce less aggressive M&A activity, and therefore less waste and fewer write-downs of acquired assets. While it may seem contradictory in an age of rising distributions to simultaneously expect material balance sheet improvement, that's not really the case. It's more a matter of quality and clarity. Less value destructive activity associated with the era of ultra-low rates will leave room for better balance sheets and greater distributions. Yes, those companies that were paying dividends only because money was cheap will struggle, but they will be more than offset by the cash nexus bringing numerous genuine new or newly material payers into the dividend universe.

Access to development capital will be one critical way to distinguish among companies in this new environment. It is not much of an exaggeration to say that any company with a pulse and a post office box could raise debt or equity over the past decade. SPACs are too good of an example. They were, as the Dire Straits song goes, literally "Money for Nothing." Less than a year after the return of risk to the stock market, they have all but disappeared. The more serious and general issue will be which companies will be able to finance the big infrastructure projects of the post-neoliberal economic "rebuild". While utilities with regulated returns should be able to greenlight their ambitious plans, other enterprises dependent on large development projects without the benefit of regulated returns will have a harder time accessing capital to finance those designs. In this case, fewer actors likely mean stronger and more successful ones. That is another reason for investors to shift their gaze from the income statement to the balance sheet.

CONSIDER BUSINESS MODEL CHANGES

Conglomerates and vertically integrated enterprises have been out of favor for decades. Minor divisions of large businesses are regularly spun off or sold to "unlock" shareholder value. Outsourcing all but the most core business functions has become common among large corporations. Consider, for example, the Boeing Company. Decades ago, it manufactured aircraft. Now it just assembles them. In the globalist neoliberal paradigm, that shift to assembling items in a just-in-time, lowest cost global supply chain made sense. It no longer does. As a result, Boeing and many other large businesses will be spending time and resources bringing their efforts back in house, creating at least partially vertically integrated operations that they can better control. While the issue of outsourcing–insourcing may not be directly related to the risk-rate trajectory that is the main thread running through this work, it is directly related to the parallel shifting balance between efficiency and efficacy in business. With the move toward the latter, I would expect to see companies want to own more of their upstream and have a greater stake in their downstream. That will likely mean lower overall margins and certainly involve higher working capital, but those entities will be able to offer greater efficacy in their operations and resiliency in times of crisis. They will be paying more to get more. In the end, that approach will be rewarded in the stock market.

Look as well for potentially changing definitions of public services and public goods. It is a perennial question in regard to internet provision. Will the new political economy tip the scales and push those services into the regulated realm? That's not out of the realm of possibility. For capital-intensive industries such as the telecom providers of underlying internet services, becoming regulated in return for guaranteed returns might be a worthwhile trade-off. In addition, the incentives within the recently enacted Inflation Reduction Act (2022) narrow the gap between the government and infrastructure enterprises, with a broader definition of the latter.

What about new technologies, especially those that promise—as all their promoters say—"disruption"? How important is it to find the next Microsoft or Google? It's as important as it has always been. The history of past disruptive technologies generally shows the stock market's initial over-enthusiasm is followed by adoption of the new technology. Trying to find the next Amazon is deeply ingrained in the *esprit* of the capital markets and in American capitalism in general. I would not dissuade anyone from pursuing that activity. The issue, as in many aspects of life, is degree and balance. From an investment perspective, the cashflow-focused investor leans heavily in the direction of established companies. That's natural. It is not in their nature to go unicorn hunting. So investors need to segment their portfolios, leaving a small portion focused on searching for exotic animals, while the rest is allocated to successful cash-distributive businesses.

PREPARING FOR THE RETURN OF VALUE

Traditionally defined "value investing" has struggled in recent years as growth stocks and momentum investors dominated the landscape. Declining risk rates during this period contributed to the demise of value. Why bother with underpriced "old economy" companies when unicorns and Big Tech were available for the asking? What opportunities might have existed on the margins have been neutralized by quantitative investors quickly closing any discrepancies in book (value) to price. That metric no longer has much utility. And the economy in general has changed. The book value of net tangible assets and retained earnings—once keystones in the exercise—has been deemed less significant than it had been in earlier generations. As a result, finding "undervalued" businesses in a classic Benjamin Graham fashion has become vastly more difficult, and perhaps no longer even relevant. In contrast, new companies, without long histories or the ability for their stocks to be parsed into "factors" by the computers, have come to the fore and dominated the marketplace for investors.

Will value investing make a comeback? If it does, it seems unlikely to be based on a discount to book value, with a catalyst in the offing to correct the mispricing. But the return of risk and the resumption of a cash nexus between investor and company will lead to a resurgence of finding good "values" in the stock market. I choose to define that value in terms of the absolute and relative price of distributable income streams. Other conservative investors may define a good value in other ways. But the return of proper risk measures will, I believe, create numerous attractive investment options for value-oriented investors in the years ahead.

I expect to see many of those opportunities in the less cyclical parts of the economy, including and without prejudice companies characterized as "new economy." My personal forecast is for a renaissance in an old economy classic: utilities. Utility stocks have fallen sharply in the past two years as rising rates have put pressure on their balance sheets and created competitors for their income streams. But their role in powering the digital economy, the internet of things, and the carbon transition is undeniable. By the time you read this account, they may or may not still be priced as good values, but I expect to see plenty of other values emerge throughout the stock market as investors adjust to the new paradigm of risk and reward.

CARE ABOUT CORPORATE GOVERNANCE

The stock market is an exercise in investment at a previously unfathomable scale. That achievement is offset partially by usually reasonable agency costs—most notably corporate management—necessary to achieve that scale. That is a remarkable outcome of the capital markets and should be applauded. There is no need to rail against agency costs in general. But they need to be taken seriously. That is, investors should care about and, to the extent possible, participate in corporate governance. For the past two decades, it has been particularly easy to ignore holding management accountable because structural tailwinds—especially declining risk rates—have made the oversight unnecessary in all but the most serious cases of CEO overreach and Board "undersight." With those tailwinds now diminished, and the political economy shifting away from more aggressive corporate behavior, it is once again time to consider corporate governance as a significant component of the investment equation.

The current ESG framework offers one platform for doing so. Whether or not ESG in its present format succeeds in tipping the balance away from the free reign management has had in recent decades, investors need to take proxy voting and corporate engagement seriously. I have specific interests and concerns—compensation packages associated with cashflow rather than share prices, split chairman and CEO roles, voting on major capital allocation decisions, etc. There are other issues that attentive investors will want to pursue. But no longer will it be acceptable to toss away the proxy ballots. That period is over.

***

These five considerations are far from exhaustive, but they may be useful starting points for investors, analysts, and portfolio managers to approach the challenge of investing in a new capital markets paradigm. The overarching theme of this work, and of my own analytical framework going forward, is to consider how the end of declining risk and interest rates will impact corporate behavior and investors in the years and decades ahead. There may be many other answers, but these questions can be the starting point.

CONCLUSION

In a book written more than a decade ago, I wrote that "we are in the midst (actually at the end) of a 25-year period when most company owners broke ranks with history and did not demand cash distributions from their investments." And I ended that treatment by making an assertion presented as a question:

> What is the likelihood that the present environment of low interest rates, low equity risk premiums, and frequent trading is sustained or accentuated even further versus the probability that our capital markets revert to a situation where money costs something, equities are thought to carry some risk, and therefore company owners and managers skew the return pattern toward cash payments?[1]

In terms of timing, I was clearly wrong, at least a dozen years early. But now that interest rates have stopped falling, the likelihood of a change in investment practices seems much greater. The paradigm shift represents a re-establishment of standard, cash-based

DOI: 10.4324/9781003292272-12

investing relationships common throughout the business world and many stock markets outside the United States. This book then serves as a periodic reminder of what "normal" is, and why it is likely to return. *This time, it turns out, is not different.* While stock markets have always been characterized by the opportunity for and the temptation of more speculative approaches, the extent and duration of the recent diversion from the long-term norm are so great that it has encompassed entire careers and is assumed to be both correct and enduring.

My good (or was it bad?) fortune was to have entered the profession in the midst of this anomaly. For most of the past two decades, being a dividend investor in a stock market has constituted a not quite solitary but a distinctly minority pursuit. Zigging when most everyone else has been zagging has come to constitute the defining characteristic of my investment career. If even a small portion of the forecasts in the second half of this book comes to be, this distinction may diminish. Indeed, I might well find myself with a lot more competition. When the cash nexus returns to the U.S. stock market, many more market participants will end up engaging in the type of investment activity that has characterized the minority of dividend-focused investors for the past several decades. For instance, conservative investors who have struggled in recent decades finding value stocks will have an additional factor—current or prospective distributable cashflows—to assist them in finding appropriate investments.

Growth stocks and their more risk-oriented investors will also face the challenge of the cash nexus. Those companies that can pay will, even if only modest amounts; those that can't had better have a plan to get to cash positive and do it quickly. The multi-decade patience of investors in enterprises such as Amazon to get large enough and have enough scale to finally pay shareholders will be exhausted. In that context, the overlap between general stock market investing and dividend investing will expand greatly. In focusing on cash returns to understand future expected total return, dividend investing as a distinct exercise may well fade into obscurity, at least until the next anomalous period of investing culture—from whatever source and in whatever form—arrives.

Just as important, if not more, will be the broader changes resulting from the end of the global neoliberal order. The entire enterprise of stock market investing in the United States has had a nearly 100-year period of generally benign political, social, and regulatory circumstances. The American Century was well represented by and partly generated by our prosperous capital markets. If that ease of operation and growth continues into another century, we shall be quite fortunate. If it is to do so, investors and companies will need to shift away from the paradigm that has dominated the past several decades—the often-hollow "financialization" of stock market activity—toward a more traditional, productive, and transparent cash basis for capital deployment, measurement, and valuation.

When exactly that occurs remains to be determined. To judge by the stock market as this book goes to press in the late summer of 2023, the paradigm shift has been deferred. Risk is back, and the market has rocketed upward. The S&P 500 Index's dividend yield has been pushed back toward 1.5%. Artificial Intelligence is the latest reason to justify an anything-goes investing climate. While it may still be a matter of when the paradigm shift occurs, it is not a matter of if. The end of the global neoliberal order and interest rates (and risk rates) hitting rock bottom in 2020 mean the prior paradigm cannot be sustained. The good news for investors is that 2023's deferral gives them more time to position themselves accordingly.

NOTE

[1] Daniel Peris, *Strategic Dividend Investor* (New York: McGraw-Hill, 2011), 25, 151.

Bibliography

BOOKS

Berle, Jr., Adolf, and Gardiner Means, *The Modern Corporation and Private Property* (New York: The MacMillan Company, 1932).

Brittain, John A., *Corporate Dividend Policy* (Washington, DC: Brookings Institution, 1966).

Chancellor, Edward, *The Price of Time: The Real Story of Interest* (New York: Atlantic Monthly Press, 2022).

Dimson, Elroy, Paul Marsh, and Mike Staunton, *Triumph of the Optimists: 101 Years of Global Investment Returns* (Princeton: Princeton University Press, 2002).

Frankfurter, George M., Bob G. Wood Jr., with James Wansley, *Dividend Policy: Theory and Practice* (San Diego: Academic Press, 2003).

Gilbert, Lewis D., *Dividends and Democracy* (Larchmont, NY: American Research Council, 1956).

Goetzmann, William N., *Money Changes Everything: How Finance Made Civilization Possible* (Princeton: Princeton University Press, 2016).

Goodman, George, "Adam Smith," in *The Money Game* (New York: Random House, 1968).

Kahneman, Daniel, *Thinking Fast and Slow* (New York: Farrar, Straus, & Giroux, 2011).

Peris, Daniel, *The Strategic Dividend Investor* (New York: McGraw-Hill, 2011).

Peris, Daniel, *The Dividend Imperative* (New York: McGraw-Hill, 2013).

Peris, Daniel, *Getting Back to Business* (New York: McGraw-Hill, 2018).

Piketty, Thomas, *Capital in the Twenty-First Century* (Cambridge, MA: Cambridge University Press, 2014).

Reamer, Norton and Jesse Downing, *Investment: A History* (New York: Columbia Business School Publishing, 2016).

Shiller, Robert J., *Narrative Economics: How Stories Go Viral and Drive Major Economic Events* (Princeton: Princeton University Press, 2019).

Solomon, Ezra, *The Theory of Financial Management* (New York: Columbia University Press, 1963).

Statman, Meir, *Finance for Normal People* (New York: Oxford University Press, 2017).

Thaler, Richard H., *Misbehaving: The Making of Behavioral Economics* (New York: W. W. Norton & Company, 2015).

Weatherall, James Owen, *The Physics of Wall Street: A Brief History of Predicting the Unpredictable* (New York: Houghton, Mifflin, Harcourt, 2013).

ARTICLES

Allen, Franklin and Roni Michaely, "Payout Policy," in G.M. Constantinides, M. Harris, and R. Stulz, eds. *Handbook of the Economics of Finance*, Vol. 1 (Amsterdam: Elsevier, 2003), 339–422.

Asness, Clifford, Todd Hazelkorn, and Scott Richardson, "Buyback Derangement Syndrome," *Journal of Portfolio Management*, Vol. 44, no. 5 (Spring 2018), 50–57.

Baker, H. Kent, Gail E. Farrelly, and Richard B. Edelman, "A Survey of Management Views on Dividend Policy," *Financial Management*, Vol. 14, no. 3 (Autumn 1985), 78 84.

Baker, H. Kent and Gary E. Powell, "Determinants of Corporate Dividend Policy: A Survey of NYSE Firms," *Financial Practice and Education*, Vol. 10, no. 4 (2000), 29–40.

Bernstein, Peter L., "Dividends: The Puzzle," *Journal of Applied Corporate Finance*, Vol. 9, no. 1 (Spring 1996), 16–22.

Bernstein, Peter L., "Dividends and the Frozen Orange Juice Syndrome," *Financial Analysts Journal*, Vol. 61, no. 2 (March–April 2005), 25–30.

Bhattacharya, Sudipto, "Imperfect Information, Dividend Policy, and 'the Bird in the Hand' Fallacy," *The Bell Journal of Economics* (Spring 1979), 259–270.

Black, Fischer, "The Dividend Puzzle," *The Journal of Portfolio Management*, Vol. 2, no. 2 (Winter 1976), 5–8.

Black, Fischer, "Why Firms Pay Dividends," *Financial Analyst Journal*, Vol. 46, no. 3 (May–June 1990), 5.

Brav, Alon, John R. Graham, Campbell R. Harvey, and Roni Michaely, "Payout policy in the 21st Century," *Journal of Financial Economics*, Vol. 77 (2005), 483–527.

Darling, Paul G., "The Influence of Expectations and Liquidity on Dividend Policy," *Journal of Political Economy*, Vol. 65, no. 3 (June 1957), 209–224.

DeAngelo, Harry and Linda DeAngelo, "The Irrelevance of the MM Dividend Irrelevance Theorem," SSRN 680855 (2005), published subsequently as Harry DeAngelo & Linda DeAngelo, "The Irrelevance of the MM Dividend Irrelevance Theorem," *Journal of Financial Economics* (February 2006), 293–315.

DeAngelo, Harry, Linda DeAngelo, and Douglas Skinner, "Corporate Payout Policy," *Foundations and Trends in Finance*, Vol. 3, nos. 2–3 (2008), 95–287.

Denis, David J., Diane K. Denis, and Atulya Sarin, "The Information Content of Dividend Changes: Cash Flow Signaling, Overinvestment and Dividend Clienteles," *The Journal of Financial and Quantitative Analysis*, Vol. 29, no. 4 (December 1994), 567–587.

Easterbrook, Frank, "Two Agency-Cost Explanations of Dividends," *American Economic Review*, Vol. 74, no. 4 (September 1984), 650–659.

Fama, Eugene F. and Harvey Babiak, "Dividend Policy: An Empirical Analysis," *Journal of the American Statistical Association*, Vol. 63, no. 324 (December 1968), 1132–1161.

Fama, Eugene F. and Kenneth R. French, "Disappearing Dividends: Changing Firm Characteristics or Propensity to Pay?" *Journal of Financial Economics*, Vol. 60, no. 1 (April 2001), 3–43.

Feldstein, Martin S. and Jerry Green, "Why Do Companies Pay Dividends?" *The American Economic Review*, Vol. 73, no. 1 (March 1983), 17–30.

Frankfurter, George M. and Bob G. Wood, Jr., "The Evolution of Corporate Dividend Policy," *Journal of Financial Education*, Vol. 23 (Spring 1997), 16–33.

Gordon, Myron J., "Dividends, Earnings and Stock Prices," *The Review of Economics and Statistics*, Vol. 44 (1963), 99–105.

Gordon, Myron J. and Eli Shapiro, "Capital Equipment Analysis: The Required Rate of Profit," *Management Science*, Vol. 3, no. 1 (October 1956), 102–110.

Harkavy, Oscar, "The Relation Between Retained Earnings and Common Stock Price for Large, Listed Corporations," *The Journal of Finance*, Vol. 8, no. 3 (September 1953), 283–297.

Hartzmark, Samuel M. and David H. Solomon, "The Dividend Disconnect," *The Journal of Finance*, Vol. 74, no. 5 (October 2019), 2153–2199.

Israel, Ronen, Joseph Liberman, Nathan Sosner, and Lixin Wang, "Should Taxable Investors Shun Dividends?" *The Journal of Wealth Management* (Winter 2019), 49–69.

Jensen, Michael C., "Agency Costs of Free Cash Flow, Corporate Finance, and Takeovers," *The American Economic Review*, Vol. 76, no. 2 (May 1986), 323–329.

Jensen, Michael C. and William H. Meckling, "Theory of the Firm: Managerial Behavior, Agency Costs and Ownership Structure," *Journal of Financial Economics*, Vol. 3 (1976), 305–360.

Kahneman, Daniel and Amos Tversky, "Prospect Theory: An Analysis of Decision Under Risk," *Econometrica*, Vol. 47, no. 2 (1979), 263–291.

Kose, John and Joseph Williams, "Dividends, Dilution, and Taxes: A Signaling Equilibrium," *Journal of Finance*, Vol. 40, no. 4 (September 1985), 1053–1070.

Krein, Julius, "The Value of Nothing: Capital vs. Growth," *American Affairs*, Vol. 5, no. 3 (Fall 2021).

Le Bris, David, William N. Goetzmann, and Sebastien Pouget, "The Present Value Relation Over Six Centuries: The Case of the Bazacle Company," *Journal of Financial Economics*, Vol. 132, no. 1 (April 2019), 248–265.

Lintner, John, "Distribution of Incomes of Corporations Among Dividends, Retained Earnings, and Taxes," *The American Economic Review*, Vol. 46, no. 2 (May 1956), 97–113.

Mann, Steven V., "The Dividend Puzzle: A Progress Report," *Quarterly Journal of Business and Economics*, Vol. 28, no. 3 (Summer 1989), 3–35.

McQuarrie, Edward F., "Introducing a New Database of 19th Century Railroads Before Cowles and Macaulay," SSRN 3011486 (2021).

McQuarrie, Edward F., "New Bank and Transportation Stock Indexes From 1793 to 1871, With Comparisons Across Region and Sector, and Against Prior Indexes," SSRN 3480838 (2021).

McQuarrie, Edward F., "Stocks for the Long Run? Sometimes Yes, Sometimes No.," SSRN 3805927 (2021).

McQuarrie, Edward F., "When Do Corporate Bond Investors Earn a Premium for Bearing Risk? A Test Spanning the Great Depression of the 1930s," SSRN 3740190 (2020).

Miller, Merton H. and Franco Modigliani, "Dividend Policy, Growth, and the Valuation of Shares," *The Journal of Business*, Vol. 34, no. 4 (October 1961), 411–443.

Miller, Merton H. and Kevin Rock, "Dividend Policy Under Asymmetric Information," *Journal of Finance* (September 1985), 1031–1051.

Modigliani, Franco, and Merton H. Miller, "The Cost of Capital, Corporation Finance and the Theory of Investment," *The American Economic Review*, Vol. XLVIII, no. 3 (June 1958), 261–297.

Peris, Daniel, "The Retreat of Dividends and the Changing Nature of the Stock Market," *American Affairs*, Vol. VI, no. 3 (Fall 2022), 3–22.

Schmelzing, Paul, Staff Working Paper No. 845, "Eight Centuries of Global Real Interest Rates, R-G, and the 'Suprasecular' Decline, 1311–2018," *Bank of England Staff Working Paper No. 845* (January 2020) via. www.bankofengland.co.uk/working-paper/2020/eight-centuries-of-global-real-interest-rates-r-g-and-the-suprasecular-decline-1311-2018

Walter, James E., "Dividend Policies and Common Stock Prices," *The Journal of Finance*, Vol. 11, no. 1 (March 1956), 29–41.

SERIALS

Commercial and Financial Chronicle
Financial Review
Moody's Analyses of Investment
Moody's Manual of Corporation Securities

ON-LINE DATABASES

Shiller, Robert, www.econ.yale.edu/~shiller/data.htm (n.d.).

S&P Global, www.spglobal.com/spdji/en/indices/equity/sp-500/#overview Additional Info, Index Earnings tab.

St. Louis Federal Reserve Bank, https://fred.stlouisfed.org/ and https://fraser.stlouisfed.org/

OTHER WEB-BASED SOURCES

Benz, Christine, www.morningstar.com/articles/619888/making-your-investment-policy-statement, originally published in 2013.

Chen, Yin and Roni Israelov, "Income Illusions: Challenging the High Yield Stock Narrative," (June 2023), https://ndvr.com/journal/income-illusions

Kelso Institute, https://kelsoinstitute.org/louiskelso/kelso-paradigm/who-what-and-why/

Ritholtz, Barry, www.bloomberg.com/opinion/articles/2020-04-24/why-you-re-not-one-of-the-world-s-great-investors?sref=vBm6bz3t, originally published in 2020.

TotalEnergies, https://totalenergies.com/system/files/documents/2023-04/EN_TotalEnergies_launches_its_annual_capital_increase_reserved_for_employees.pdf

Acknowledgments

My thanks to Ian Bangor and Abigail Barr for their research assistance. I also want to thank Stephen Crane, Chris Donahue, Lawrence J. Fossi, James P. Garland, Jared Hoff, Jon Lukomnik, and Mike Tucker for their comments and suggestions on earlier versions of the text. John Allison rendered additional copyediting support. The team at Routledge, Rebecca Marsh and Lauren Whelan, made the publication process very smooth. All errors of fact, interpretation, logic, or sloppy writing are mine. My greatest debt is to my family, who has graciously tolerated me writing "just one more book." As I have promised in the past, this one is the last.

Selected, condensed excerpts from the first half of this work appeared as "The Retreat of Dividends and the Changing Nature of the Stock Market," in *American Affairs*, Vol VI, no. 3 (Fall 2022), 3–22. I am grateful to the editor, Julius Krein.

Unless otherwise attributed, all post-1962 aggregate stock market data come from the Compustat database of S&P Global Market Intelligence. I am grateful for the courtesy they extended me to use their data. In regard to that Compustat data, please note the following disclosure:

Index

Note: Page numbers in *italics* indicate figures and page numbers in **bold** indicate tables on the corresponding pages.

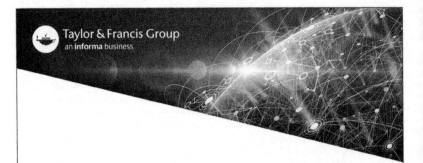